# FOR BREW FREAKS, BEAN GEEKS, AND THE SIMPLY CURIOUS ...

# SCOTTISH
## INDEPENDENT
# COFFEE
# GUIDE

the **INSIDER'S GUIDE TO SPECIALITY COFFEE VENUES AND ROASTERS**

★★★★★★★★★★

Nº3

Salt Media, 5 Cross Street, Devon, EX31 1BA.
**www.saltmedia.co.uk**
Tel: 01271 859299
Email: ideas@saltmedia.co.uk

**Salt Media *Independent Coffee Guide* team:**
Nick Cooper, Catherine Courtenay, Lucy Deasy,
Kathryn Lewis, Abi Manning, Tamsin Powell, Jo Rees,
Rosanna Rothery, Christopher Sheppard, Dale Stiling,
Katie Taylor and Mark Tibbles.
**Design and illustration:** Salt Media
**Typeset:** Brooklyncoffe, DIN Pro and Cheap Pine

**A big thank you to the *Independent Coffee Guide*
committee** (meet them on page 148) for their expertise
and enthusiasm, **our headline sponsors** Cimbali,
KeepCup and Schluter, **and sponsors** Almond Breeze,
Cakesmiths, Mossgiel Farm and Shibui Tea.

Coffee shops, cafes and roasters are invited to be
included in the guide based on meeting criteria set by
the committee, which includes a high quality coffee
experience for visitors, use of speciality beans and
being independently run.

For information on the Ireland, The North and North
Wales, and South West and South Wales *Independent
Coffee Guides,* visit:

**www.indycoffee.guide**
🐦 @indycoffeeguide
📷 @indycoffeeguide

**30** PAPERCUP COFFEE
ROASTERS

# Contents

When 2017 delivered a knockout year for the Scottish speciality coffee scene, little did we know that 2018 was revving up to be even greater.

The number of new venues continues to soar and indie coffee shop closures are almost unheard of. This ever-increasing thirst for quality coffee is testament to the pioneers who paved the way for speciality in this now caffeine-rich country.

It's been full steam ahead in the roasting revolution too, with some game-changing outfits hitting the scene and a record number of cafes stocking their grinders with own-roasted beans.

The barista's armoury of brewing gear has also developed – check out our feature on page 26 for the low-down on the latest kit and roasting trends.

And while speciality continues to flourish in Edinburgh and Glasgow, there's a growing scene out in the wilds. Read all about it on page 14.

Another exciting development was being awarded Best Coffee Book in Scotland in the *Gourmand World Cookbook Awards* for last year's guide.

We reckon it's going to be another killer year for coffee and, armed with your new *Scottish Indy Coffee Guide*, promises to be filled with one-of-a-kind experiences and inspiring new finds.

**Kathryn Lewis**

Editor

*Indy Coffee Guides*

🐦 @indycoffeeguide

📷 @indycoffeeguide

**The world's first barista standard reusable cup.
Manufactured and assembled in the UK.**

keepcup.com

# Wild Coffee

Grab an Edinburgh or Glasgow city map, stick a pin in at random, and if it doesn't land near a speciality coffee shop, consider yourself unlucky.

But often overlooked is the growing crop of indies pushing quality coffee in the wilds. We spoke to three cafe owners about serving speciality in the sticks ...

# MIKE HAGGERTON
## HABITAT CAFE, ABERFELDY

'When we relocated from London to the Highlands in 2012, good coffee was sparse in Scotland and speciality almost unheard of outside the cities,' says Mike.

'My wife Jan and I spent 18 months looking for a location, and when we found Aberfeldy it immediately felt right. However, launching Habitat wasn't easy. There were numerous complaints to the council when we applied for planning permission and local business owners scoffed at us for opening a cafe without having done so before.

'Being a newcomer in a small Highland town was never going to be plain sailing but as the community saw how hard we were working things became easier.

'There were some steep learning curves in adjusting to rural life. After a few months of opening bright and early for the morning rush, I found that it doesn't exist here and I couldn't create it. Eventually I accepted that to survive in the Highlands you need to adapt – the Highlands won't adapt to you.

'The influx of visitors to Aberfeldy is extremely seasonal too, and following the first year it became apparent that I would have to plan and budget around summer takings that were almost ten times that of winter.

'I've worked hard to put together a comprehensive brew bar at Habitat, but that doesn't mean we pander to a hipster crowd. I may have a beard and filament bulbs above the counter but a lot of our loyal locals are over 50. Some city shops have boasted of 'educating' their customers but our approach has always been to 'interest'. We combine a bit of brewing theatre with our own excitement to charm and delight our customers with great tasting coffee.

'The best part about running a rural coffee shop? During my 10 minute commute to work I pass a hauntingly beautiful castle, frequently see clouds in the valley below, and dodge a handful of deer crossing our track. As a former London dweller, I think of those benefits daily.'

## 'ON MY WAY TO WORK I PASS A HAUNTINGLY BEAUTIFUL CASTLE AND DODGE A HANDFUL OF DEER CROSSING OUR TRACK'

# JONNY AND ALI ASPDEN
## THE COFFEE APOTHECARY, UDNY

'It wasn't our intention to bring speciality to rural Aberdeenshire when we opened a coffee shop in Udny's former post office in 2014,' admits Jonny.

'We knew we wanted to make coffee – as well as everything else at the cafe – to the best possible standard, but we had no idea how to brew and serve speciality and our location meant that there was no one around to teach us. I would hate to now drink the coffee we served in the first few weeks; it was only through hours of research and determination that we learnt the trade.

'The brewing kit such as V60 and Chemex confused some of the locals at first but we've managed to make filter less daunting. It's great to see people's interest in speciality develop: they often start with a latte, maybe go to a cafetiere next as it's familiar and then ask someone else what they're drinking. Then they're converted.

'Unlike the coffee shops in the cities we don't have hundreds of potential customers walking past every day, but word of mouth is amazing and the amount of people who go out of their way to make a trip is humbling. We also have more time to get to know our customers and, instead of people rushing to get to work, we can have a chat and catch up with our regulars who have become friends.

'There are downsides to our location: staffing is a battle. We've wanted to expand The Apothecary's food offering and opening hours into the evening for a long time, but hiring the right people for the role is tricky. Finding individuals who are willing to work full time in hospitality is harder in a rural area. What's more, it takes time to train someone to craft coffee to our high standards.

'On a more positive note, it's been great to see speciality expand from the cities. While we had no one to seek advice from when we were starting out, we've recently been able to answer questions and help out new coffee shops opening outside of Glasgow and Edinburgh.'

**'I WOULD HATE TO NOW DRINK THE COFFEE WE SERVED IN THE FIRST FEW WEEKS'**

# JAMIE FLETCHER
## CAORA DHUBH COFFEE COMPANY, ISLE OF SKYE

'I thought converting the locals to speciality coffee was going to be the biggest challenge,' laughs Jamie, 'but it turns out that transporting a three group La Marzocco from Udny to the Isle of Skye in the back of my car was much harder.'

'When Caora Dhubh opened in 2017 the whole village turned out to support the cafe. The odd person thought I was a chancer for charging £2.50 for a takeaway coffee at first, but I was amazed at how quickly everyone got behind the concept.

'We've got a good crop of regulars now. There are students fresh from uni who are used to the speciality standards of the cities, but there are also some loyal followers like the retired forestry commissioner and local shopkeeper, who swear by the good stuff. Skye is a big island and we've even got a couple of guys who travel over an hour from the north for a takeaway.

'Getting the coffee to the cafe can be a minefield. It's expensive to transport beans roasted in Edinburgh to Skye quickly. Other factors can also impact the delivery of the beans and we've had weekends where we've had to close because we don't have any coffee. There's no one to service our machine locally either, and if we want to get an engineer out to the island it costs a fortune.

## 'GETTING THE COFFEE TO THE CAFE CAN BE A MINEFIELD'

'But being part of the community far outweighs the niggles. The site for the coffee shop is a locally-managed project so our rent goes straight back into the village. We've got great links with other businesses on the island too: some of the local B&Bs and pubs give their guests vouchers for the cafe and a local lady takes our coffee grounds and distributes them to gardeners. You don't get that sense of community in big cities.'

# SCHLUTER

SINCE 1858

Speciality green coffee suppliers

— since 1858 —

# Purpose.
# Passion.
# Progress.

# DIY coffee roasting

You've kitted out your kitchen with the latest brewing gear, nailed a killer Chemex recipe and sussed out the steam wand, but are you ready to roast beans at home? We roped in a few industry insiders to find out what it takes

# Green bean 101

You'll need to start with some green beans, but not all greens are equal: origin, process and varietal all affect the fruits of your labour when roasting. Don't know where to start? Don't sweat – we got the green bean 101 from Ross Nicholson, speciality importer at Schluter

## CONSISTENCY IS KEY

'When selecting green beans, you need to consider their consistency,' explains Ross.

'Single origin coffees are usually graded and screened to be of uniform size and density, so should roast consistently in one batch.

'If you're looking to blend coffees which have been processed or prepared differently, however, they will often require a different treatment in the roast to get the most out of their flavour potential.'

## PROCESS = PROFILE

'Coffee cherries from the same tree in Ethiopia can produce wildly contrasting cups depending on the way in which they've been processed,' says Ross. 'This will affect how the beans behave in the roast.'

**Washed process** Cherry pulp is removed mechanically before the beans are fermented and washed to remove all the remaining fruit. The finished profile is delicate and refined, and tends to present citrus and floral notes like lavender, lemon and hops. Their high altitude growth means a good injection of heat is needed to permeate the dense beans and ensure an even roast.

**Natural process** This involves drying the coffee cherries in the sun on raised beds, allowing the sugars in the fruit to transfer into the bean. This process produces more jammy flavours, with bags of juicy fruits and a creamy body. Natural coffees require a more gentle treatment to ensure the sugars caramelise into a pleasantly sweet profile.

## BUYING GREENS

'Finding a small enough supply for the home roaster can be a challenge as importers tend to distribute large volumes,' says Ross. 'We import green beans from all around the world for speciality roasters but we also work with IKAWA to supply home roasters. Many speciality roasters will also sell green beans in smaller batches, so contact your local roasters for advice.'

# Flash in the pan

It doesn't take a professional chef to fry an egg or roast a chicken, but surely roasting coffee can't be as simple as turning on the oven?

'*Our roastery started out as a kitchen pan, hob and handful of green beans,*' explains Neil Buchan of Kinross' Unorthodox Roasters. '*We couldn't afford to go straight in with a commercial roaster so experimenting in the pan was an easy and affordable way to go about it.*'

## Domestic dilemmas

'*Roasting coffee in a pan is a fun way to experiment, but from a sensory and quality point of view it's not a great method of roasting,*' says Lisa Lawson, qualified SCA trainer and founder of Dear Green Coffee in Glasgow. '*To produce great tasting coffee you need to be able to control variables such as temperature.*'

While you may think that using the oven instead of a pan solves the temperature conundrum, it also has drawbacks: '*As the coffee cannot be agitated it will scorch and roast unevenly. There would be no way to manipulate flavour either, as there is little control over the heat transfer or air flow,*' says Lisa.

So what are the options if you're still keen to see the process through from green bean to cup?

'*Unfortunately, it's going to take a bit of cash to craft great tasting coffee at home – a brand new commercial single barrel roaster could set you back thousands. However, there are some affordable alternatives. At Dear Green we're rolling out roasting courses on a 1kg Probat. We also use an IKAWA – their recently launched home edition is opening new doors for burgeoning roasters.*'

---

### UNORTHODOX'S GUIDE TO PAN ROASTING

**1.** Heat a large, dry pan on the hob. Add a handful of green beans and start a timer.

**2.** Maintain a high heat and continually stir the beans so they don't burn.

**3.** Once the beans start to turn from green to cereal colour and begin to lightly smoke, drop the heat and continue to stir.

**4.** At around the 8 minute mark, the coffee will begin to pop. This is called 'first crack'.

**5.** Turn down the heat and roast for a further 2 minutes while the chaff is expelled and coffee develops.

**6.** It's up to you when to stop the roasting process – colour and smell are good indicators, or play it safe with 2-3 minutes after first crack.

**7.** Remove the beans from the heat and stir in a metal sieve.

**8.** Grind, brew and luxuriate in caffeinated smugness.

# IKAWA power

Roasting coffee from your phone for your Saturday morning hit may sound outré, yet keen connoisseurs across the country are cooking up beans in their kitchen with this bit of kit

'THE MACHINE FOLLOWS A PRE-DEFINED ROAST CURVE, ALLOWING USERS TO WATCH THE ROAST'

'**U**ntil recently, many coffee lovers had been deterred from roasting at home as it was perceived as messy and complex,' explains IKAWA's Alex Georgiou. 'So we designed the IKAWA At Home to make the process super accessible.'

Roasting 50g of green beans at a time, the compact IKAWA roaster has long been used by professional roasters to road-test samples and experiment with new blends. The recent introduction of a home edition allows speciality enthusiasts to take their interest to the next level.

'The method is simple: select a recipe on the app. The machine then follows the pre-defined roast curve, allowing the user to watch the roast happening and appreciate the aromas. The whole process is no longer than nipping to the nearest speciality shop for a fresh bag of beans.'

'To make it even easier, we've curated a selection of great coffees from the most iconic origins on the planet, which we stock on our website. Each coffee has its own distinct characteristics to help roasting freshers appreciate the breadth of flavours and understand how roasting can accentuate different aspects.'

## ROASTING GLOSSARY

**Chaff** A papery substance that's shed from the beans during roasting and which must be removed.

**First crack** During roasting, when high pressure inside the bean causes it to split.

**Origin** The specific region of a country where a bean is grown.

**Process** The process by which the green bean has been dried. This can be washed, natural or honey.

**Varietal** The variety of bean. They each have specific characteristics.

**PGS** (Perfect Grinding System) integrated management system.

*For the highest quality coffee and the greatest possible flexibility.*

Customisable 4.3" touch screen display.

*To create a set of custom settings every time.*

Compact design and hopper with smart shape.

*To improve visibility from the counter and simplify refill and cleaning.*

Work cycle integrated with Inverter motor.

*To ensure low consumption and constant performance.*

New LaCimbali Elective

# PERFECT COFFEE STARTS THIS WAY.

The quality of a coffee is never just about the bean.
It's never just about the roasting process, and neither is it ever just about that first sip.
The perfect coffee is an idea in constant evolution.
Welcome to the world of **Elective**.

# The innovators

From frozen bean shots to slot roasting to hydraulic mobile espresso machines, speciality coffee continues its relentless pursuit of perfection through innovation. Here's what's new in the Scottish scene – and beyond

# Frozen bean shots

Freezing beans has been a controversial topic in the speciality world for some time, with coffee pros clashing over its impact on freshness and whether ice crystals alter flavour. But one bold barista is rolling out frozen shots for a different reason at his Edinburgh coffee shop.

*'Our intention at Cairngorm is always to improve consistency,'* explains owner Robi Lambie. *'For this reason, we're freezing coffee to give us a more stable starting point when we grind which, in turn, gives us a more consistent grind profile.'*

While vacuum sealing and freezing prevents short term ageing without impacting on flavour, how does sending roasted beans sub-zero affect the grind?

## 'WE'VE STARTED FREEZING COFFEE BEANS TO GIVE US A MORE STABLE STARTING POINT'

*'We want a reasonably thin spread between course and fine grinds to ensure that our coffee is extracting at the same time and not offering up unwanted flavours,'* says Robi. *'Starting with frozen beans means the structure shatters in a more even way than ambient temperature beans. With this more consistent grind profile, we aim to extract more from our sample without the risk of over extracting.*

*'We don't have a conclusive solution for how to implement freezing within a commercial environment and, until we develop a less wasteful process, we're not vacuum sealing the beans. Instead, we're pre-dosing (weighing) individual shots each afternoon for every espresso we expect to sell the next day, and freezing these overnight. We've added a sunken freezer to the counter – next to our EK 43 grinder – which keeps the shots cold enough to be effective.'*

And the verdict? *'We're not scientists; we're baristas,'* stresses Robi. *'A lot of our experiments have been relatively relaxed. We do, however, seem to be developing more balance and sweetness than ever before.'*

# Rent -a- roaster

An increasing number of coffee shop owners and baristas want to serve customers their own-roasted beans. However, eye-wateringly expensive roastery start-up costs have priced many aspiring bean alchemists out of the roasting realm – until now.

Picking up on the interest in roasting, and knowing first-hand the expense of setting up a roastery, experienced coffee buffs Todd and Courtney of The Good Coffee Cartel launched Glasgow's first slot roasting service at the end of 2017.

*'Setting up a space that allows cafes and consumers to roast their own beans was always part of the big plan behind The Good Coffee Cartel,'* says Todd. *'Buying a roaster is a massive investment, so we wanted to create somewhere people could buy time on our roaster and craft their own coffee.'*

Todd and Courtney not only rent out the roastery space on Cornwall Street, they also offer their expertise in equipment, green bean buying and designing badass branding to create coffee that's unique to each cafe.

*'We start with a consultation to work out which flavour profiles reflect the business, then we help them choose which green beans to buy, based on their ideas and the harvest calendar,'* continues Todd.

## 'TODD AND COURTNEY LAUNCHED GLASGOW'S FIRST SLOT ROASTING SERVICE'

It's not just professional espresso slingers getting in on the roasting action either; the guys have also opened up slot roasting to keen amateur coffee fans. The half and full day experiences allow novices to experiment on the sample roaster and learn the principles of roasting before creating their own bespoke blend to take home.

*'We want to make roasting accessible for all. No pretension – just fun,'* smiles Todd.

# killer kit

Get ready for some seriously geeky new gear

## ESPRESSO KOMPRESSO

The 'world's first portable pourover coffee maker', the Cafflano, changed the on-the-go coffee game when it was launched in 2014, bringing top-notch filter to festival goers and off-piste adventurers. And now its little brother, the Kompresso, is making waves in espresso.

Mobile brews are hitting barista heights with this clever piece of kit which uses a hydraulic system (designed to retain high pressure) to create machine-standard espresso on-the-move.

## PRESSING ISSUE

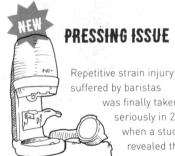

Repetitive strain injury suffered by baristas was finally taken seriously in 2014 when a study revealed that tamping coffee (the process of compacting coffee into the espresso basket) had the potential to cause injury behind the bar. With the word out that tamping can take its toll, an increasing number of coffee shops have turned to gadgets to tackle wrist strain.

The PuqPress (a precision tamping device) is appearing on coffee counters across the country, and is designed to prevent injury and improve consistency in the cup. Using sensors, the compact kit allows baristas to dial in an exact tamp pressure and ensures the ground coffee is perfectly level in the basket.

## MILK ON TAP

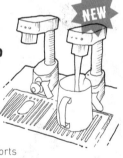

Aussies have inspired our speciality scene and its environmental efforts (KeepCup started down under, FYI), and their latest export sees the next step in coffee shop sustainability.

The Juggler Cafe Milk Tap System is designed to reduce milk waste, plastic bottles and energy expenditure. A tap built straight into the bar, the Juggler dispenses refrigerated milk in pre-dosed measures into the jug which saves barista time and is also at an optimum temperature for texturing. Even better, storing the milk in 10 litre bladders instead of bottles saves on plastic as well as energy waste from opening and closing the fridge. #win

# How to use the guide

65 HULA
JUICE BAR

# CAFES

Coffee shops and cafes where you can drink top-notch speciality coffee. We've split Scotland into areas to help you find places near you.

# ROASTERS

Meet the leading speciality coffee roasters in Scotland and discover where to source beans to use at home. Find them after the cafes in each area.

# MAPS

Every cafe and roastery has a number so you can find them either on the area map at the start of each section, or on the detailed city maps.

# MORE GOOD STUFF

Discover **MORE GOOD CUPS** and **MORE GOOD ROASTERS** at the back of the book.

**Don't forget to let us know how you get on as you explore the best speciality cafes and roasteries.**

# WWW.INDYCOFFEE.GUIDE

🐦 @indycoffeeguide  📷 @indycoffeeguide

Your
*adventure*
*starts*
*here*

**02** CAORA DHUBH
COFFEE COMPANY

# Maps

## KEY

Cafe

Roaster

More Good Cups

More Good Roasters

Coffee Training Facility

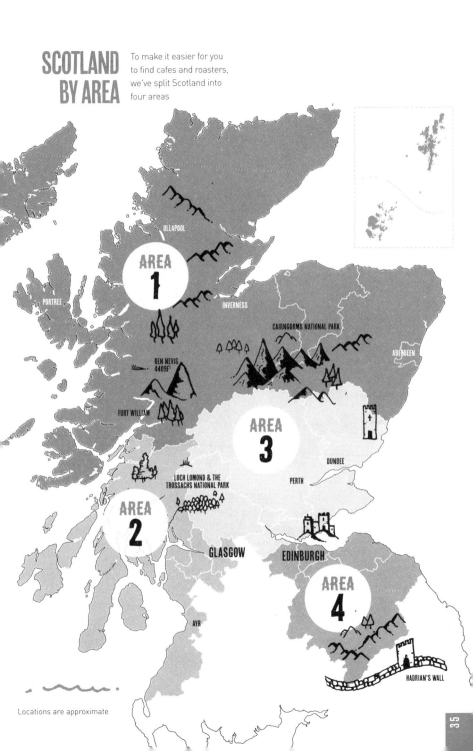

# SCOTLAND BY AREA

To make it easier for you to find cafes and roasters, we've split Scotland into four areas

ULLAPOOL

PORTREE

**AREA 1**

INVERNESS

CAIRNGORMS NATIONAL PARK

ABERDEEN

BEN NEVIS
4409FT

FORT WILLIAM

**AREA 3**

DUNDEE

LOCH LOMOND & THE TROSSACHS NATIONAL PARK

PERTH

**AREA 2**

GLASGOW

EDINBURGH

**AREA 4**

AYR

HADRIAN'S WALL

Locations are approximate

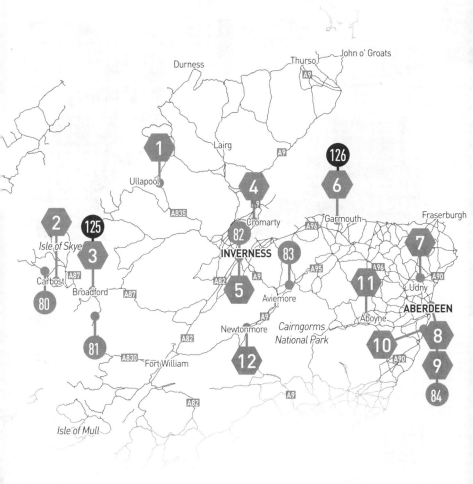

## CAFE

1 The Ceilidh Place
2 Caora Dhubh Coffee Company
3 Cafe Sia
4 Slaughterhouse Cafe
5 Little Bird Coffee House
6 Speyside Coffee Roasting Co.
7 The Coffee Apothecary
8 The Cult of Coffee
9 Foodstory
10 Shamrock and Thistle
11 Spider on a Bicycle
12 Ralia Cafe

## MORE GOOD CUPS

80 Bog Myrtle Skye
81 Cafe 1925
82 Velocity Cafe
83 Nethy House Cafe & Rooms
84 The Craftsman Company

## MORE GOOD ROASTERS

125 Skye Roastery
126 Speyside Coffee Roasting Co.

All locations are approximate

# №1. THE CEILIDH PLACE

12-14 West Argyle Street, Ullapool, Ross-shire, IV26 2TY

Photos: David Brown Photographer

On the 500 trail and overlooking Loch Broom at Ullapool, The Ceilidh Place has got the location sorted.

Happily, things are as inspiring inside as out, because this cafe/restaurant/bar/hotel/music venue/bookshop (it's a lot of things to a lot of people) is a cheerful and cosy retreat from the often harsh conditions outdoors.

Creativity courses through everything here: there's art galore (often by local artists), a great selection of books in the rooms and regular music events in the cafe and bar.

### INSIDER'S TIP VISITING ON A BUDGET? STAY IN THE CEILIDH PLACE BUNKHOUSE OUT FRONT

All of this activity is fuelled by Red Stag espresso – roasted by Scottish roasters Glen Lyon – and served in the usual styles, although owner Beccy says they're investigating filter and pourover options too.

Don't miss the homebaked scones and goodies and, if you're staying for dinner, finish with a cheeseboard with crumbly homemade oatcakes (with a whisky, naturally) followed by an espresso. When in Rome and all that …

ESTABLISHED
1970

KEY ROASTER
Glen Lyon
Coffee Roasters

BREWING METHOD
Espresso,
cafetiere

MACHINE
Conti

GRINDER
Mahlkonig K30

OPENING HOURS
**Mon-Sun**
8am-11pm

 Gluten FREE

 BEANS AVAILABLE INSTORE

 ALTERNATIVE MILK

 WIFI

 CYCLE FRIENDLY

 OUTDOOR SEATING

 FAMILY FRIENDLY

 DISABLED ACCESS

---

**www.theceilidhplace.com**   T: 01854 612103

f The Ceilidh Place   🐦 @theceilidhplace   📷 @1970ceil

# MAP №2. CAORA DHUBH COFFEE COMPANY

Carbost, Isle of Skye, IV47 8SR

This tiny little takeaway must have one of the best coffee shop locations in the UK: on the shore of Skye's Loch Harport, with dramatic views of the Cuillins. It's rural, it's remote – and it's right opposite the Talisker Distillery.

Don't visit expecting a Highlands-style tea room though; Caora Dhubh is all clean-lined and design-driven modernism, with its black sheep motif turning up in all manner of funky merch.

### INSIDER'S TIP PICK UP A QUIRKY BLACK SHEEP T-SHIRT ON YOUR VISIT – YOU WON'T FIND ONE ANYWHERE ELSE

Having opened in 2017, it's still early days for owner Jamie Fletcher and team, who are currently serving up Edinburgh-roasted Artisan Roast beans as espresso based drinks thanks to their Mythos One/La Marzocco grinder/machine combo.

Grab a cup to-go, pair it with a slab of something scrummy, and wander outside to breathe in the exhilarating scene as you sip. Then take a tour of the distillery and finish up the hill at The Oyster Shed for a lunch of oysters fresh from the loch. Talk about sucking out the marrow of life …

**ESTABLISHED**
2017

**KEY ROASTER**
Artisan Roast
Coffee Roasters

**BREWING METHOD**
Espresso

**MACHINE**
La Marzocco
FB70

**GRINDER**
Mythos One

**OPENING HOURS**
**Mon-Sat**
10am-5pm

*Gluten* **FREE**

**BEANS** AVAILABLE
 INSTORE

 ALTE RNA TIVE **MILK**

 **WIFI**

 **OUTDOOR** seating

**DISABLED** **& ACCESS**

---

**www.caoradhubh.com**  T: 01478 640666
f Caora Dhubh Coffee Company  ◎ @caoradhubh

# ᴹᴬᴾ**3.** CAFE SIA

Ford Road, Broadford, Isle of Skye, IV49 9AB

Once you're over the bridge and onto Skye, you're just a hop, skip and a jump from your first island coffee destination: Cafe Sia.

Specialising in own-roasted coffee and wood-fired pizza (cooked in an oven that owner Tom drove home to Skye from Pisa), it's no surprise that this diner-style restaurant is usually rammed. So get here early if you want to get a table, or visit mid-morning for a decent flattie and hang on 'til lunch.

### INSIDER'S TIP: 17 WHISKIES AND BEERS FROM SIX MICRO BREWERIES GET THE PARTY STARTED

The espresso also makes an appearance on the homemade Italian-style gelato menu as dairy-free espresso gelato, and also turns up in the coffee shake.

It's the coffee and malt whisky tasting menu that really sorts the men from the boys though. Choose from a double shot of espresso paired with a wee dram, push the boat out with two, or call a taxi and go for the full tasting session with coffee and three whiskies for £20.

**ESTABLISHED**
2014

**KEY ROASTER**
Skye Roastery

**BREWING METHOD**
Espresso, filter

**MACHINE**
Fracino
Contempo x 2

**GRINDER**
Mahlkonig

**OPENING HOURS**
**Mon-Sun**
10am-9pm
(seasonal
opening hours)

 Gluten FREE

 BEANS AVAILABLE INSTORE

 ALTERNATIVE MILK

 WIFI

 CYCLE FRIENDLY

 OUTDOOR Seating

 FAMILY FRIENDLY

 DISABLED ACCESS

 BRING YOUR OWN Cup

---

**www.cafesia.co.uk**   T: 01471 822616

f Cafesiaskye   🐦 @cafesiaskye   📷 @cafesia_skye

# MAP № 4. SLAUGHTERHOUSE CAFE

Marine Terrace North, next to Cromarty to Nigg ferry slipway, Cromarty, Highland, IV11 8XZ

The traffic passing most cafes usually consists of cars, bikes and pedestrians – here you're as likely to spot a dolphin.

An unassuming cabin right on the slipway for the Cromarty to Nigg ferry, Slaughterhouse Cafe already harbours an impressive stash of single origin coffees, despite only opening last year.

Alongside the Dark Woods roasts, the cafe also features its own Slaughterhouse blend: a fusion of Brazilian, Indian and Ethiopian beans. You can buy the coffee in bags to take away and the house roast has gone down so well that the owners behind the shop plan to open their own roastery soon.

## INSIDER'S TIP TRY SEAL SPOTTING WITH A FLAT WHITE AND WEDGE OF BROWN AND BLONDE BROWNIE

A carefully selected range of edibles sourced from quality producers includes sourdough from Wild Hearth Bakery in Comrie and muffins from Cromarty's Factor's House B&B.

There are plenty of reasons to stop at the historic Highlands town, but a visit to Slaughterhouse for the view, the dolphins and the coffee make it a must.

**ESTABLISHED**
2017

**KEY ROASTER**
Vandyke Brothers

**BREWING METHOD**
Espresso, pourover

**MACHINE**
La Marzocco Linea PB

**GRINDER**
Mazzer Kold, Mahlkonig EK 43

**OPENING HOURS**
**Mon-Sun**
9am-2pm
(seasonal hours in winter)

BEANS AVAILABLE INSTORE

ALTERNATIVE MILK

CYCLE FRIENDLY

OUTDOOR SEATING

DISABLED ACCESS

BRING YOUR OWN CUP

T: 07494 492695

🐦 @vandykebros  📷 @vandykebros

# №5. LITTLE BIRD COFFEE HOUSE

Ironworks Venue, 122b Academy Street, Inverness, IV1 1LX

**B**y night this lively venue plays host to the likes of Kasabian and Van Morrison, while by day it showcases famous names of the caffeinated kind.

Setting up shop in Inverness's popular music venue, Ironworks, Little Bird Coffee House features speciality rock stars such as Koppi, Five Elephant and Workshop.

Headliners at the coffee shop include The Barn and Extract, with scientist-turned-barista Julie bigging up the high grade beans and talking freshers through the brew bar options.

### INSIDER'S TIP THE TOASTED STORNOWAY BLACK PUDDING BAGEL WITH BRIE AND CRANBERRY IS EPIC

*'In a city with no coffee scene, we take time to talk and share our passion with fellow coffee lovers in the hope of educating people about speciality coffee – without sounding pretentious,'* she explains.

Since opening in 2015, Jay and Julie have attracted an appreciative audience for their food, local bakes and bimonthly music sessions. They're also happy to share the limelight with co-creatives – a collaboration with a soapmaker sees grounds transformed into coffee-scented suds.

**ESTABLISHED**
2015

**KEY ROASTERS**
Extract Coffee Roasters

**BREWING METHOD**
Espresso, V60, AeroPress, Chemex

**MACHINE**
La Marzocco Linea PB

**GRINDER**
Mahlkonig K30 Air

**OPENING HOURS**
**Mon-Fri**
8.30am-2.30pm
**Sat** 10am-2pm
(extended in summer)

 *Gluten* FREE

 BEANS AVAILABLE INSTORE

 ALTERNATIVE MILK

 WIFI

 CYCLE FRIENDLY

 OUTDOOR seating

 FAMILY FRIENDLY

 DISABLED ACCESS

BRING YOUR OWN Cup

---

T: 07740 124659

f Little Bird Coffee House  🐦 @lbcoffeehouse  📷 @littlebirdcoffee

# MAP No 6. SPEYSIDE COFFEE ROASTING CO.

Garmouth Hotel, South Road, Garmouth, Moray, IV32 7LU

They're an entrepreneurial bunch at Speyside. After a downturn in pub trade, Jody and Grant Spence decided to realise their dream of coffee roasting: something they'd toyed with since Jody worked at a roastery in New Zealand.

The pair turned one of the ground floor rooms of their Garmouth Hotel pub into a cafe in March 2017, installing a roaster so they could serve their own beans.

It's been a hit with the customers and spawned all manner of spin-offs, from the counter of homebakes (the coffee cake is a winner) to a collaboration with local distillery El:gin (from Elgin, geddit?) producing Moray Mocha which is served in the espresso martinis. They're also working with a craft brewery on a coffee ale.

## INSIDER'S TIP YOU'RE IN WHISKY COUNTRY HERE, SO PAIR YOUR COFFEE WITH A WEE DRAM FROM THE BAR

Currently, it's a one roast situation – chocolatey, Brazilian speciality grade beans roasted for espresso – which locals, whisky tourists and cyclists make a detour for, drinking the coffee at the cafe as well as taking beans away for home brewing.

**ESTABLISHED**
2017

**KEY ROASTER**
Speyside Coffee Roasting Co.

**BREWING METHOD**
Espresso, filter, cafetiere

**MACHINE**
La San Marco

**GRINDER**
Mazzer,
La San Marco

**OPENING HOURS**
**Tue-Sun**
11am-4pm

Gluten FREE

BEANS AVAILABLE
INSTORE

ALTE RNA TIVE MILK

WIFI

CYCLE FRIENDLY

OUTDOOR seating

FAMILY FRIENDLY

DISABLED ACCESS

www.speysidecoffee.co.uk   T: 01343 870226

f Speyside Coffee Roasting Co.   @speysidecoffee   @speysidecoffee

# MAP 7. THE COFFEE APOTHECARY

Udny, Ellon, Aberdeenshire, AB41 7PQ

**A**ny coffee fan would be stoked to chance upon this speciality pit-stop on a rural highway a few miles north of Aberdeen.

Imagine pulling in for a quick cuppa and loo break, expectations set at zero, only to find coffee tasting boards and speciality beans prepared and served in different styles.

### INSIDER'S TIP THE CAFE IS NOW OPEN SEVEN DAYS A WEEK, SO THERE'S NO RISK OF A WASTED ROAD TRIP

You'd be met with a flawless flat white, care of Apothecary's Cobblestone house espresso (berry fruit, caramel and almond notes), a perfect pourover (served on an elegant wooden board) and extensive coffee info and tasting notes.

On the food front, pre-packed roadside sarnies are eschewed in favour of freshly cooked homemade dishes such as quality burgers served in pretzel buns, pulled pork wraps, Thai chicken salad and soup of the day.

The vibe is contemporary and rustic, with lots of hanging filament bulb lighting and the notable polished-pennies-in-resin loo flooring, while owners Jonny and Ali and their team are super friendly and knowledgeable.

**ESTABLISHED**
2014

**KEY ROASTER**
Artisan Roast
Coffee Roasters

**BREWING METHOD**
Espresso,
Kalita Wave,
cafetiere

**MACHINE**
La Marzocco
Linea PB ABR,
Marco SP9

**GRINDER**
Mahlkonig K30,
Mahlkonig EK 43

**OPENING HOURS**
**Mon-Sun**
9am-4pm

 Gluten FREE

 BEANS AVAILABLE INSTORE

 ALTERNATIVE MILK

 WIFI

 CYCLE FRIENDLY

OUTDOOR seating

FAMILY FRIENDLY

 DISABLED ACCESS

 BRING YOUR OWN cup

www.thecoffeeapothecary.co.uk    T: 01651 842253

f The Coffee Apothecary    🐦 @udnyapothecary    📷 @thecoffeeapothecary

# MAP 8. THE CULT OF COFFEE

28 Esslemont Avenue, Aberdeen, AB25 1SN

The team at Cult are revelling in their mission to further develop Aberdeen's speciality scene.

As the only purely coffee-focused spot in the area, the guys are keen to break down bean barriers, talking customers through the coffee on offer and introducing brew classes (due to start later this year).

The house espresso is Artisan Roast's Janszoon blend and there are also regularly changing filters. In the summer months you can cool off with a cold brew – made in house and triple filtered.

### INSIDER'S TIP IN A CARBY CONUNDRUM? THE CAKE SLIDER HAS FIVE DIFFERENT CHOICES

The interior is fitted out with simple wood, tiles and splashes of colour, with plenty of room for Cult's bill of music and storytelling events. A wood burner creates a great atmosphere in winter, as does the music playlist which is painstakingly created by the gang.

With a Michelin-trained pastry chef at the helm, you know the cakes and baked goodies will be top-notch, and those scones when warm out of the oven ... phwoar.

**ESTABLISHED**
2017

**KEY ROASTER**
Artisan Roast
Coffee Roasters

**BREWING METHOD**
Espresso,
Clever Dripper,
cold brew

**MACHINE**
La Marzocco
Linea PB

**GRINDER**
Mazzer Major,
Mahlkonig EK 43

**OPENING HOURS**
**Mon-Sat**
8.30am-5pm
**Sun** 10am-5pm

 Gluten FREE

 BEANS AVAILABLE INSTORE

 ALTERNATIVE MILK

 WIFI

 CYCLE FRIENDLY

 OUTDOOR SEATING

 FAMILY FRIENDLY

 DISABLED ACCESS

 COFFEE COURSES

f The Cult of Coffee   @the_cult_of_coffee

# №9. FOODSTORY

11-15 Thistle Street, Aberdeen, AB10 1XZ

This particular Foodstory is a little like a fairytale: there were hopes (of opening a fantastic cafe), there was jeopardy (when the lease they had taken out on their original building turned out to be worthless), true love (finding the premises they're now in) and dreams come true (the plan worked, customers loved it and they've grown beyond their wildest expectations).

The latest chapter has seen the launch of the new wholefoods shop upstairs (which also hosts yoga, life drawing classes and community workshops), the building of a swanky kitchen and bakery, and the development of a horsebox for an on-the-go Foodstory fix.

### INSIDER'S TIP: SUNDAY IS FUNDAY (AND PANCAKE DAY) FROM 11AM-3PM

Downstairs, the mostly vegan/veggie cafe is much loved for its fresh homemade food (especially the vegan mac 'n' cheese), the quirky, contemporary styling and, of course, great coffee.

Using beans roasted by Glasgow's Dear Green, along with a guest list from all over, the team serve espresso based drinks alongside V60, Chemex and batch brew, and are enjoying playing with their shiny new Linea PB.

**ESTABLISHED**
2013

**KEY ROASTER**
Dear Green
Coffee Roasters

**BREWING METHOD**
Espresso, V60,
Chemex,
batch brew

**MACHINE**
La Marzocco
Linea PB

**GRINDER**
Mahlkonig EK
43, Mythos One,
Mazzer Super
Jolly, Mazzer
Kold, Mazzer
Tanzania

**OPENING HOURS**
**Mon-Thu**
8am-9pm
**Fri** 8am-10pm
**Sat** 9am-9pm
**Sun** 11am-3pm

Gluten FREE

BEANS AVAILABLE
INSTORE

ALTERNATIVE MILK

WIFI

CYCLE FRIENDLY

FAMILY friendly

BRING YOUR OWN Cup

---

www.foodstorycafe.co.uk   T: 07753 225962

f FoodStory   🐦 @foodstorycoffee   📷 @foodstoryscotland

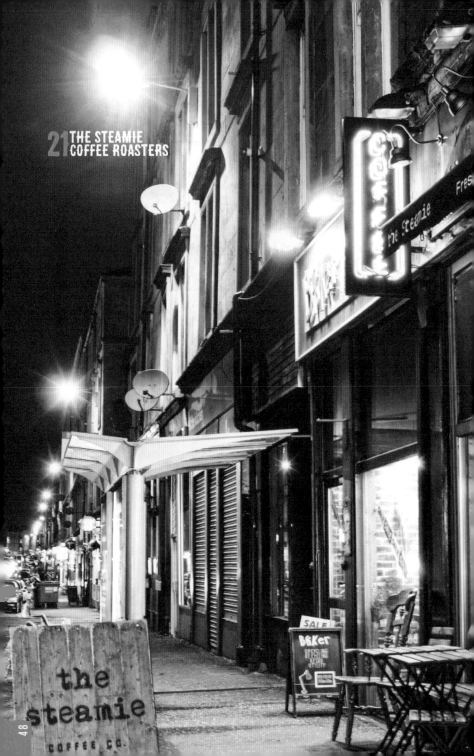

# MAP 10. SHAMROCK AND THISTLE

6 Arbuthnott Place, Stonehaven, Aberdeenshire, AB39 2JA

If the name hasn't already given it away, the menu of crêpes and waffles named after Irish and Scottish castles should reveal the blend of heritages behind Shamrock and Thistle.

Gerard and Sarah Browne only launched in Stonehaven in 2017, but the husband and wife team have already built a loyal following for their top-notch coffee which is crafted from an armoury of brewing gear and single origin beans.

### INSIDER'S TIP PICK UP A BAG OF SACRED GROUNDS BEANS FOR THE ROAD

The colourful mural on the back wall gives freshers an introduction to the world of speciality coffee, while Sarah and Gerard are always up for answering questions about the seasonal line-up from Angus roaster, Sacred Grounds.

Walter and Wilma (the waffle irons, obvs) take care of appetites with a sweet and savoury bill of batter beauties.

Momentous munchies such as the Balmoral – smoked salmon, cream cheese, spinach and egg – are crafted with locally sourced ingredients, while freshly folded crêpes stuffed with all manner of naughties tempt visitors to stay a little longer.

ESTABLISHED
2017

KEY ROASTER
Sacred Grounds
Coffee Company

BREWING METHOD
Espresso,
Chemex, V60,
AeroPress,
Moccamaster
batch brew

MACHINE
La Marzocco
Linea PB

GRINDER
Mazzer Robur E,
Mahlkonig EK 43

OPENING HOURS
**Mon Fri**
9.30am-5pm
**Sat** 10am-5pm
**Sun** 11am-4pm

Gluten FREE

BEANS AVAILABLE
INSTORE

ALTERNATIVE MILK

CYCLE FRIENDLY

FAMILY FRIENDLY

DISABLED ACCESS

BRING YOUR OWN Cup.

T: 07734 218704

f Shamrock and Thistle

# MAP 11. SPIDER ON A BICYCLE

Station Square, Aboyne, Aberdeenshire, AB34 5HX

The revival of Aboyne's former train station into a speciality coffee shop was much anticipated by the area's caffeine enthusiasts and a great intro for those unfamiliar with the high grade stuff.

Sisters Hollie and Emma Petrie roped in the whole family when they took over the listed building in 2016, bringing in dad to build the copper countertop and mum to re-upholster the quirky furnishings which fill the high-ceilinged space.

## INSIDER'S TIP
**BRUNCH IS AN ALL-DAY THING ON SUNDAY – GET YOUR FIX OF EGGS, AVO AND SMOKED SALMON**

The hands-on approach hasn't changed now that the cafe hums with the hiss of the steam wand and cheery chatter of local coffee converts. Emma bakes the haul of carby beauties which have garnered their own fanbase – the carrot and ginger cake is particularly popular – while the brekkie and lunch dishes are also made from scratch in the kitchen.

Fuelling the gluttony is a line-up of single origin beans from Papercup Coffee in Glasgow. Sample the seasonal selection as espresso based brews before bagging the latest batch to take home.

**ESTABLISHED**
2016

**KEY ROASTER**
Papercup Coffee Roasters

**BREWING METHOD**
Espresso

**MACHINE**
La Marzocco Linea Classic

**GRINDER**
Nuova Simonelli

**OPENING HOURS**
**Tue-Sat**
8.30am-4.30pm
**Sun**
9am-4.30pm

Gluten FREE

BEANS AVAILABLE / INSTORE

ALTERNATIVE MILK

WIFI

CYCLE FRIENDLY

OUTDOOR SEATING

FAMILY FRIENDLY

DISABLED ACCESS

---

**www.spideronabicycle.com**

f Spider on a Bicycle   @spideronabicycle

# 12. RALIA CAFE

Ralia, Newtonmore, Inverness-shire, PH20 1BD

Fergus the Hairy Coo (a Kev Paxton sculpture) who hails visitors to this A9 stop-off has to be the most Instagrammed bovine in Scotland. The artwork is just one of the welcoming faces at this unique coffee shop housed in a former Tourist Information Centre.

Run by Robin and Sheila Lambie, Ralia is an oasis for drooping-at-the-wheel drivers craving a speciality break. And not only is it perfect for a perk-up of espresso or filter (the couple recently started to roast their own), there's also sustenance in the form of sarnies and soups, to fuel you for the journey ahead.

### INSIDER'S TIP POP NEXT DOOR TO THE HAIRY COO GIFT SHOP

Everything is sourced in Scotland wherever possible, with bread from Inverness's Harry Gow, chocolate cookies baked in Kingussie, shortbread from Loch Lomond's Chrystal's and ice cream from Perthshire.

Robin and Sheila have made it their mission to think of everything flagging travellers might possibly need at this Perth to Inverness pit-stop including iPads for public use, a free printing service and mobile chargers to use and buy – not forgetting bags of coffee beans so you can relax with a beautiful brew on reaching your destination.

**ESTABLISHED**
2005

**KEY ROASTER**
Ralia

**BREWING METHOD**
Espresso, filter,
Marco Filter
Shuttle

**MACHINE**
Sanremo Zoe

**GRINDER**
Mazzer Robur

**OPENING HOURS**
**Mon-Sun**
8am-8pm
(summer)
**Mon-Sun**
8am-6pm
(winter)

Gluten FREE

BEANS AVAILABLE
INSTORE

ALTERNATIVE MILK

WIFI

CYCLE FRIENDLY

OUTDOOR Seating

FAMILY FRIENDLY

DISABLED ACCESS

BRING YOUR OWN Cup

**www.ralia.co.uk**   T: 01540 670066
f Ralia Café

Area &

19 BLACK PINE
COFFEE CO.

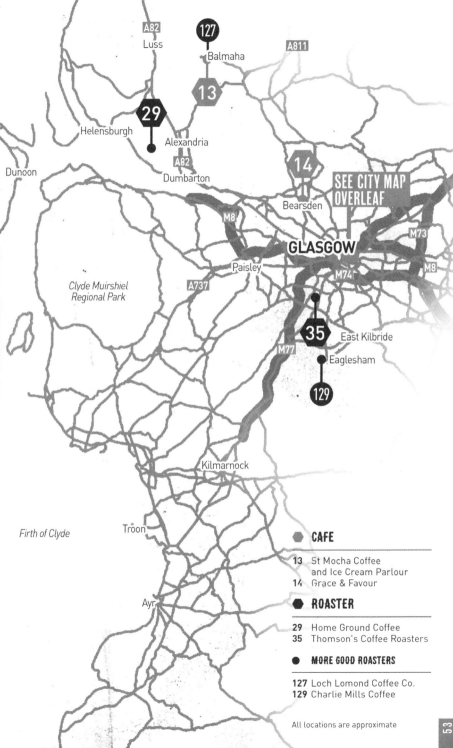

CAFE

13 St Mocha Coffee
and Ice Cream Parlour
14 Grace & Favour

ROASTER

29 Home Ground Coffee
35 Thomson's Coffee Roasters

MORE GOOD ROASTERS

127 Loch Lomond Coffee Co.
129 Charlie Mills Coffee

All locations are approximate

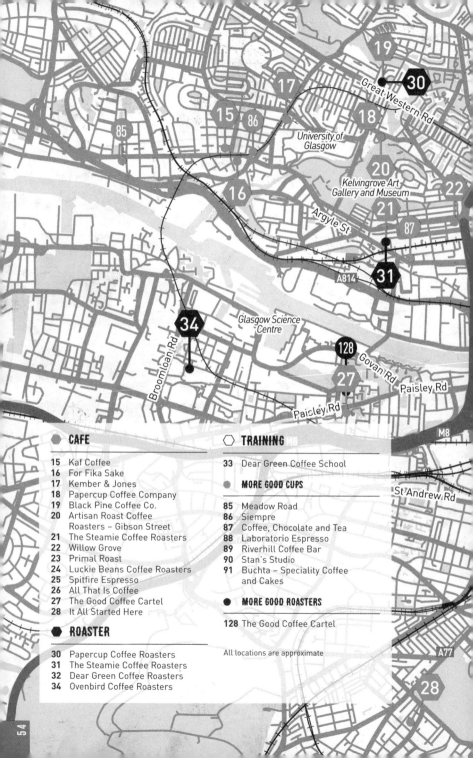

## CAFE

15  Kaf Coffee
16  For Fika Sake
17  Kember & Jones
18  Papercup Coffee Company
19  Black Pine Coffee Co.
20  Artisan Roast Coffee
    Roasters – Gibson Street
21  The Steamie Coffee Roasters
22  Willow Grove
23  Primal Roast
24  Luckie Beans Coffee Roasters
25  Spitfire Espresso
26  All That Is Coffee
27  The Good Coffee Cartel
28  It All Started Here

## ROASTER

30  Papercup Coffee Roasters
31  The Steamie Coffee Roasters
32  Dear Green Coffee Roasters
34  Ovenbird Coffee Roasters

## TRAINING

33  Dear Green Coffee School

### MORE GOOD CUPS

85  Meadow Road
86  Siempre
87  Coffee, Chocolate and Tea
88  Laboratorio Espresso
89  Riverhill Coffee Bar
90  Stan's Studio
91  Buchta – Speciality Coffee
    and Cakes

### MORE GOOD ROASTERS

128  The Good Coffee Cartel

All locations are approximate

# MAP № 13. ST MOCHA COFFEE SHOP AND ICE CREAM PARLOUR

Main Street, Balmaha, Loch Lomond, Glasgow, G63 0JQ

Founded by brothers Stuart and David Fraser, this little gem can be found alongside the award winning Oak Tree Inn in Balmaha.

'Once visited, never forgotten' should be its tagline, as the quirky space is hugely memorable thanks to the inventive use of old bits of coffee machine kit which decorate the shop, along with light fittings made from glass bottles.

It seems there's no end to the brothers' coffee ambitions as, in addition to opening a second outlet across the water at Luss Pier (for summer sipping), they've also started roasting their own beans at Balmaha on a Giesen W15A. You can sample the fruits of their labour or choose from the selection of guest roasts from the likes of Charlie Mills, Unorthodox and Dear Green.

### INSIDER'S TIP TRY AN ESPRESSO OVER A SCOOP OF HOMEMADE ST MOCHA VANILLA ICE CREAM

For precision tamping, the baristas use PuqPresses at both sites, and this machine geekery is nicely balanced by the serving of coffee in cups designed by local artist Wil Freeborn.

**ESTABLISHED**
2014

**KEY ROASTER**
Loch Lomond Coffee Co.

**BREWING METHOD**
Espresso

**MACHINE**
La Marzocco Linea PB

**GRINDER**
Mazzer Kold

**OPENING HOURS**
**Mon-Sun**
10am-6pm

---

www.stmocha.co.uk   T: 01360 870357

f St Mocha Coffee Shop & Ice Cream Parlour   🐦 @stmochacoffee   📷 @stmochacoffee

# MAP Nº 14. GRACE & FAVOUR

11 Roman Road, Bearsden, Glasgow, G61 2SR

There's a luxurious feel to this coffee shop, mainly due to its smart interior of dark wood, richly painted walls and bespoke lighting. It's certainly an easy place to relax with a Home Ground flat white.

Get there for breakfast or brunch to enjoy homemade granola, french toast with bacon, or eggs stornoway with black pudding and creamy hollandaise. Hang around too long and you'll be wanting a coffee refill, plus lunch, which involves tempting sandwiches, soups, tarts and crostini.

### INSIDER'S TIP DON'T EVEN THINK ABOUT LEAVING WITHOUT TRYING THE RHUBARB MERINGUE PIE

For something sweet to go alongside your espresso, the in-house bakery provides a wide selection of cakes and scones, elegantly displayed on the counter. And if your coffee levels have peaked, there's a fine selection of loose-leaf teas available too.

Building a solid reputation for good food, great coffee and friendly service, Grace & Favour is drawing both visitors and locals to this delightful historic suburb.

ESTABLISHED
2014

KEY ROASTER
Home Ground
Coffee

BREWING METHOD
Espresso

MACHINE
La Marzocco

GRINDER
Mazzer Jolly

OPENING HOURS
**Mon-Sat**
8.30am-5pm
**Sun** 10am-5pm

 Gluten FREE

 BEANS AVAILABLE INSTORE

 ALTERNATIVE MILK

 WIFI

 OUTDOOR seating

 FAMILY FRIENDLY

  DISABLED ACCESS

www.graceandfavourcoffee.com  T: 01415 706501
f Grace & Favour  @graceandfavourcoffee

# №15. KAF COFFEE

5 Hyndland Street, Glasgow, G11 5QE

This slick new addition to Glasgow's expanding coffee scene is proof that size isn't everything.

The wee West End spot may appear unassuming to passersby (tall picture window, pared-back interior and an impressive collection of house plants), but step inside and you'll find a seriously specialist caffeine fix and edible offering to match.

Sourcing beans from small coffee roasters across the UK, Kaf founder and former Brew Lab barista – Leonora Belcher switches up the single origin offering weekly. Coffee is showcased as espresso or Kalita, and Leo has drafted in some experienced baristas.

## INSIDER'S TIP
### PICK UP BEANS AND BREWING GEAR TO KICK YOUR HOME HIT UP A NOTCH

Brunch plates and bakes receive similarly specialist attention. Chow down on house faves such as eggs benny with salsa, avo and cajun hollandaise, and lamb kofte flatbread, or go trad with a Scandi lunch plate featuring bacon, egg, cheese, new potatoes, hummus and sourdough.

The line-up of counter cakes (we're still dreaming about the salted caramel brownies) are baked in house and also available to order for your next knees up.

**ESTABLISHED**
2017

**KEY ROASTER**
James Gourmet Coffee,
Curve Coffee Roasters,
Campbell & Syme Coffee Roasters

**BREWING METHOD**
Espresso,
Kalita Wave

**MACHINE**
La Marzocco Linea EE

**GRINDER**
Mythos One,
Mahlkonig EK 43

**OPENING HOURS**
**Mon-Sat**
8am-5pm
**Sun** 9am-5pm

Gluten FREE

BEANS AVAILABLE
INSTORE

ALTERNATIVE MILK

WIFI

OUTDOOR seating

BRING YOUR OWN cup

COFFEE COURSES

---

www.kafcoffee.co.uk

f Kaf Coffee   @kafcoffee

# №16. FOR FIKA SAKE

7 Keith Street, Glasgow, G11 6QQ

A Scottish-Scandi blend of hospitality and community spirit come together at this chilled-out space, where everyone is welcome to stop by for a spot of fika.

All manner of creative folk congregate at this buzzing hub, from mums and babies tucking into lunch on the squidgy sofas to arty types at workshops upstairs and inspired locals tickling the ivories on the free-for-all piano.

### INSIDER'S TIP DON'T STOP AT COFFEE – THE VEGAN CHOC PEANUT BUTTER SPONGE MASH-UP IS TO DIE FOR

Two years in and manager Simon continues to develop the social enterprise side of the cafe, introducing life drawing classes, pottery sessions and yoga. You can even rent out the space in the evening for your own event.

And fuelling the inventive energy? Another opportunity to promote local projects: Simon's drafted in down-the-road newbies, The Good Coffee Cartel, to stock Fika's busy Mazzer. There's usually a guest filter to be explored via V60, AeroPress or Chemex too, plus a tempting cake collection at the counter.

**ESTABLISHED**
2016

**KEY ROASTER**
The Good Coffee Cartel

**BREWING METHOD**
Espresso, V60, AeroPress, Chemex

**MACHINE**
La Marzocco Linea

**GRINDER**
Mythos One

**OPENING HOURS**
**Mon** 11am-5pm
**Tue-Wed** 10am-6pm
**Thu** 10am-9pm
**Fri** 10am-7pm
**Sat-Sun** 10am-6pm

Gluten FREE

BEANS AVAILABLE INSTORE

ALTERNATIVE MILK

WIFI

CYCLE FRIENDLY

OUTDOOR SEATING

FAMILY FRIENDLY

DISABLED ACCESS

BRING YOUR OWN CUP

---

**www.forfikasake.co.uk**  T: 07851 255804
f For Fika Sake  🐦 @forfikasake  📷 @forfikasake

# 17. KEMBER & JONES

134 Byres Road, Glasgow, G12 8TD

**H**ead to bohemian Byres Road and hit up cool-as-they-come Kember & Jones; it's a West End institution.

The family-run coffee shop launched 14 years ago after Phil Kember and head chef Claire Jones worked a summer and ski season together. Since then they've added a bakery and coffee roastery to their portfolio and created one of the city's best-loved food and caffeine emporiums.

Moreish mounds of meringues and macarons on the counter make any resistance futile. Complement sweet-toothed whims with the house coffee blend: freshly roasted beans ensure a well-rounded cup with chocolatey, caramel richness, fruity notes and a sweet, long finish.

### INSIDER'S TIP
**THE WARM BANANA BREAD WITH CRÈME FRAÎCHE AND SALTED CARAMELISED PECANS IS LUSH**

A visit promises to be more than a quick fling. Make it a doughy-eyed love affair with straight-from-the-oven toast at brekkie, a decadent mid-morning cranberry scone, a lunchtime baguette stuffed with rare roast beef and emmental, and a glass of wine and something delish from the specials board as the sun goes down.

**ESTABLISHED**
2004

**KEY ROASTER**
Kember & Jones

**BREWING METHOD**
Espresso, filter

**MACHINE**
La Marzocco Linea

**GRINDER**
Mahlkonig

**OPENING HOURS**
**Mon-Fri**
8am-10pm
**Sat**
9am-10pm
**Sun**
9am-6pm

 Gluten FREE

 BEANS AVAILABLE INSTORE

 ALTERNATIVE MILK

 WIFI

 OUTDOOR seating

 FAMILY Friendly

 DISABLED ACCESS

BRING YOUR OWN Cup

---

**www.kemberandjones.co.uk**    T: 01413 373851

f Kember & Jones    🐦 @kemberandjones    📷 @kemberandjones

# MAP№ 18. PAPERCUP COFFEE COMPANY

603 Great Western Road, Glasgow, G12 8HX

A highly skilled and upbeat team of baristas serve a menu of seasonal single origins at this Great Western Road venue, which are roasted down the road at Papercup's roastery.

Guests from Europe's best roasters also make an appearance at the slow brew bar, which features V60, AeroPress and cold brew.

### INSIDER'S TIP GRAB A BAR OF PAPERCUP'S OWN CHOCCIE, CREATED WITH ARTISAN CHOCOLATIERS 88 DEGREES

The sociable lot have the same approach to the food menu as the coffee: only ethical and sustainable ingredients are sourced and served.

'Healthy without being health food', the endorphin-boosting dishes include matcha pancakes, a salt and chilli tofu sandwich and plenty of avocado-packed plates. With a focus on flavour, there are lots of veggie and vegan options too.

Community fun in the form of natural wine tastings, pop-up food nights, free cuppings and coffee training sessions ensure the good vibes flow from dawn til dusk.

ESTABLISHED
2012

KEY ROASTER
Papercup Coffee
Roasters

BREWING METHOD
Espresso, V60,
AeroPress,
cold brew

MACHINE
La Marzocco
Linea

GRINDER
Mythos One,
Ditting KR1203

OPENING HOURS
**Mon-Fri**
8.30am-6pm
**Sat-Sun**
9am-5.30pm

 *Gluten* FREE

 BEANS AVAILABLE INSTORE

 ALTERNATIVE MILK

 WIFI

 CYCLE FRIENDLY

 OUTDOOR SEATING

 FAMILY FRIENDLY

 DISABLED ACCESS

 BRING YOUR OWN CUP

COFFEE COURSES

---

www.papercupcoffee.co.uk    T: 07719 454376

f Papercup Coffee Company    🐦 @pccoffeeuk    📷 @pccoffeeuk

# ℕᵒ 19. BLACK PINE COFFEE CO.

518 Great Western Road, Glasgow, G12 8EL

A much-Instagrammed neon sign declaring 'Death Before Decaf' reveals that this new coffee shop in Glasgow's West End takes a wry approach to seriously good coffee.

Since opening in September, speciality seekers have been making pilgrimages here for the house roast (supplied by The Good Coffee Cartel) and a rotating line-up of guests: Machina, Unorthodox, Bailies and Thomson's all make appearances.

## INSIDER'S TIP
**IT'S A HAVEN FOR DOGS: A WHOLE HOST OF WEST END POOCHES REGULARLY GATHER HERE**

Exposed brickwork, a sandstone pillar and eye-catching art lend character to a space that's continually evolving as word spreads about the coffee, raw plant-based cakes from locals RAWNCHY and decadent brownies and banana bread baked by KAF.

Prop up the bar and chat over coffee recipes and brew methods with owner Pete Duthie or grab a seat next to the large south facing window. It's a great spot to linger over a laptop, literature or lecture notes while making the most of the cheery, chilled-out vibe.

**ESTABLISHED**
2017

**KEY ROASTER**
The Good Coffee Cartel

**BREWING METHOD**
V60, AeroPress, Chemex

**MACHINE**
Noveseinove LED All Black

**GRINDER**
Remidag

**OPENING HOURS**
**Mon-Fri**
8am-5pm
**Sat** 9am-5pm
**Sun** 10am-4pm

Gluten FREE

BEANS AVAILABLE INSTORE

ALTERNATIVE MILK

WIFI

OUTDOOR seating

FAMILY FRIENDLY

BRING YOUR OWN Cup

---

**www.blackpinecoffee.com**   T: 01413 349987
f Black Pine Coffee Co.   🐦 @blackpinecoffee   📷 @blackpinecoffee

# №20. ARTISAN ROAST COFFEE ROASTERS – GIBSON STREET

15-17 Gibson Street, Glasgow, G12 8NU

L aying claim to being the first speciality coffee shop in Glasgow, Artisan Roast is an alluring hideaway if you're looking for good coffee with good vibes in the city.

Weave your way through the sea of students sprawled in the eclectic collection of mismatched chairs and stools to secure a corner at this characterful hangout.

Sample a single origin espresso downstairs at an old door-turned-table, or find a cosy nook upstairs in which to read by lamplight, stealing peeks over the balcony at the caffeine alchemy going down at the brew bar.

### INSIDER'S TIP ARTISAN'S BEVY OF GONGS INCLUDES THE GLENFIDDICH SPIRIT OF SCOTLAND AWARD

Beans are sourced and roasted by the Artisan Roast team in Edinburgh (where there are three sister coffee shops), so expect lip-smackingly fresh single origins arriving hot from HQ several times a week.

This lot are keen to get the nation coffee literate, too: educate yourself by studying the filter flow chart on the blackboard above the bar and you'll be spouting speciality lingo in no time.

**ESTABLISHED**
2009

**KEY ROASTER**
Artisan Roast Coffee Roasters

**BREWING METHOD**
Espresso, V60, Chemex, AeroPress

**MACHINE**
La Marzocco FB80

**GRINDER**
Nuova Simonelli, Mazzer Major x 2

**OPENING HOURS**
**Mon-Fri**
8am-5.30pm
**Sat-Sun**
9am-5.30pm

 Gluten FREE

 BEANS AVAILABLE INSTORE

 ALTERNATIVE MILK

 WIFI

 CYCLE FRIENDLY

 OUTDOOR seating

 BRING YOUR OWN Cup

 COFFEE COURSES

---

www.artisanroast.co.uk  T: 07864 984253

f Artisan Roast Glasgow  🐦 @artisanroastgla  📷 @artisan_roast_glasgow

# 21. THE STEAMIE COFFEE ROASTERS

1024 Argyle Street, Glasgow, G3 8LX

'*People often compare The Steamie to their granny's living room*,' confesses owner Stephen Meek. The cosy vibe and homemade bakes? Maybe. The single origin Guatemalan coffee via Chemex and Colombian baked eggs with toasted soda scone? Not so much.

The absence of a bar between the baristas and customers creates an open and homely atmosphere at this Finnieston stalwart. Coffee-curious visitors quiz the crew on the latest small batch, own-roasted beans, while famished foodies get the inside info on which of the seasonal sandwiches shouldn't be missed that day.

## INSIDER'S TIP
**DON'T LEAVE WITHOUT PICKING UP A BAG OF STEAMIE BEANS FOR YOUR HOME BREW BAR**

Just like Glasgow's original steamies (communal wash houses, FYI), the cafe is a buzzing hub of local life and laughter. Hunker down with a book and a flat white in the window, stop by for a swift cold brew to-go and catch up with the super friendly team, or bring your brood for a brunch of skillet baked eggs, pimped porridge and Scottish smoked salmon and cream cheese-slathered toast.

**ESTABLISHED**
2014

**KEY ROASTER**
The Steamie Coffee Roasters

**BREWING METHOD**
Espresso, Chemex, V60, AeroPress, cold brew

**MACHINE**
La Marzocco Linea

**GRINDER**
Mythos One, Mahlkonig K30, Mahlkonig Guatemala

**OPENING HOURS**
**Mon-Fri**
8am-6pm
**Sat** 9am-6pm
**Sun** 10am-5pm

 Gluten FREE

 BEANS AVAILABLE INSTORE

 ALTERNATIVE MILK

 CYCLE FRIENDLY

 OUTDOOR seating

 DISABLED ACCESS

 BRING YOUR OWN cup

 COFFEE COURSES

---

www.thesteamie.co.uk  T: 07821 544449
f The Steamie Coffee Roasters  🐦 @the_steamie  📷 @thesteamie

# Nº**22.** WILLOW GROVE

531 Sauchiehall Street, Glasgow, G3 7PQ

The eclectic decor, quality caffeine and feel good vibes found at Glasgow's latest indie bring together owner Adele McPhee's travels under one roof.

Eight years of planning – and a couple of years slinging espresso on various machines across Australia – led to Willow Grove's launch in 2017, where Adele has captured an authentic taste of antipodean cafe culture with a killer coffee, breakfast and lunch bill.

Previously hitting the festival circuit and roasting with Alastair at Home Ground Coffee, Adele keeps the hopper happy with a custom house espresso blend from the Cardross roaster. V60 converts will also find interesting guest beans from monthly-changing roasters.

### INSIDER'S TIP COOL OFF WITH A CARDAMOM COLD BREW OR V60 ICE CREAM FLOAT

And when the all-day brunch menu kicks in on the weekend, it's avo mania at this hass-haven. Magic Poached Eggs is the brekkie of choice and marries smashed avo and lime with chopped toms, red onion and a spiced poachie on a chunky slice of granary. Waffles with pistachios and ricotta are the biz too.

During the week, sandwich specials such as fiery salt beef satisfy grumbling tums post-noon.

ESTABLISHED
2017

KEY ROASTER
Home Ground
Coffee

BREWING METHOD
Espresso, V60,
Chemex

MACHINE
Astoria Rapallo

GRINDER
Fiorenzato F83

OPENING HOURS
**Mon-Fri**
8am-6pm
**Sat** 9am-5pm
**Sun** 10am-4pm

 Gluten FREE

 BEANS AVAILABLE / INSTORE

 ALTERNATIVE MILK

 WIFI

 CYCLE FRIENDLY

 OUTDOOR SEATING

 FAMILY FRIENDLY

 DISABLED ACCESS

T: 01412 373490

f Willow Grove Coffee  🐦 @willowgrove531  📷 @willowgrovecoffee

# <sup>MAP</sup>23. PRIMAL ROAST

278 St Vincent Street, Glasgow, G2 5RL

The logo says it all: this is a prime spot for speciality sippers seeking a hit that'll take them from a prehistoric state to caffeinated cool.

An eclectic mix of clean-eating coffee fans flock to the St Vincent Street cafe, from speciality geeks to gym bods and suit-wearing lunch breakers (it's smack bang in the financial district).

Primal Roast is the brainchild of health-food enthusiast and former sous chef at the Ubiquitous Chip, Iain Walker. Armed with a spanking new Mazzer Kold grinder and bespoke blend from Dear Green (among a smorgasbord of guests including Glasgow new-kids-on-the-block, The Good Coffee Cartel), Iain and barista bro Ross dish out espresso and filter to satisfy the primal desire for caffeine.

### INSIDER'S TIP
**SEEK OUT THE HIDDEN SEATING AREA AT THE BACK OF THE CAFE**

After that sweet hit, turn your attention to the seasonally-changing menu for guilt-free gluttony that's anything but primitive: think aubergine, fennel and bean stew buddha bowl followed by a gluten-free, wheat-free, vegan slice of raw caramel cake.

**ESTABLISHED**
2016

**KEY ROASTER**
Dear Green
Coffee Roasters

**BREWING METHOD**
Espresso, V60,
AeroPress

**MACHINE**
La Marzocco
Linea

**GRINDER**
Mazzer Kold,
Baratza Encore

**OPENING HOURS**
**Mon-Fri**
7.30am-4pm
**Sat** 10am-3pm

---

**www.primalroast.com**   T: 01412 222750

f Primal Roast   🐦 @primalroast   📷 @primalroast

# MAP № 24. LUCKIE BEANS COFFEE ROASTERS

Luckie Beans Coffee Cart, Glasgow Queen Street Station, Glasgow, G1 2AF

Answering commuters' early morning cries for quality caffeine (what's the deal with the lack of good coffee at transport hubs, huh?), Luckie Beans is taking on the chains at Glasgow's Queen Street train station.

Acquiring a coffee cart with just two weeks to launch the new project, Berwick-upon-Tweed roaster Jamie McLuckie revamped the wagon – which previously dished out coffee in a South Wales bus depot and London tube station – before debuting the specialist set-up in the summer of 2016.

### INSIDER'S TIP LOOK OUT FOR A SISTER CART HITTING EVENTS AND FARMERS' MARKETS THIS SUMMER

Each morning you'll now find a clan of office workers queuing at the La Marzocco for their pre-work hit of Luckie Beans' Love Lane house blend. Its popularity means it's a purely espresso operation, though alternatives in the form of matcha lattes, hot chocolate and a couple of artisan softies are also available.

With the baristas slinging espresso until late on weekdays, you can also hit the cart on your way home and pick up beans for an out-of-office fix.

**ESTABLISHED**
2016

**KEY ROASTER**
Luckie Beans
Coffee Roasters

**BREWING METHOD**
Espresso

**MACHINE**
La Marzocco
Linea 2 AV

**GRINDER**
Mazzer Super
Jolly Electronic

**OPENING HOURS**
**Mon-Sat**
6.30am-8pm
**Sun**
8am-6.30pm

www.luckiebeans.co.uk   T: 07810 446537

f Luckie Beans Coffee Roasters   🐦 @luckiebeans   📷 @luckie_beans

# MAP 25. SPITFIRE ESPRESSO

127 Candleriggs, Merchant City, Glasgow, G1 1NP

Photos: John Cruttenden

I t's been a crazily busy year for the gang behind this maverick espresso bar and cafe in the heart of Merchant City.

As well as consistently cranking out exceptional brews for coffee buffs, owners Danny and Emily Gorton have added a new evening menu, reshuffled the speciality offering and extended the opening hours – and all while juggling their roles as new parents.

Not that you'd notice; the service is as slick and cheerful as ever. Local roaster Thomson's now takes care of the cafe's bespoke Gunnerbeans blend, while the addition of a Mythos One grinder ensures a perfect profile in every cup.

**INSIDER'S TIP** CHECK OUT THE KILLER BRUNCH BILL, INCLUDING THE GLASGOW-FAMOUS HAWKER HURRICANE

Guest roasts from the likes of The Good Coffee Cartel make an appearance too – try 'em as 12 hour cold brew.

And new evening sessions from Wednesday to Saturday have made way for a short menu of seasonal small plates. Pair dishes such as grilled dumplings and pickled sausage with local and international craft beers from the regularly updated line-up.

ESTABLISHED
2015

KEY ROASTER
Thomson's
Coffee Roasters

BREWING METHOD
Espresso,
cold brew

MACHINE
La Marzocco
FB70

GRINDER
Mythos One,
Mazzer Major,
Mazzer Super
Jolly

OPENING HOURS
**Mon-Tue**
8am-6pm
**Wed-Sat**
8am-8pm
**Sun** 10am-4pm

 Gluten FREE

 BEANS AVAILABLE / INSTORE

 ALTERNATIVE MILK

 WIFI

 CYCLE FRIENDLY

 OUTDOOR seating

 FAMILY FRIENDLY

 DISABLED ACCESS

 BRING YOUR OWN Cup

www.spitfireespresso.com   T: 07578 250105

f Spitfire Espresso   🐦 @spitfireglasgow   📷 @spitfireglasgow

# GLASGOW COFFEE FESTIVAL

HOSTED BY **Dear GREEN** Coffee Roasters Est. 2011

## THE BRIGGAIT | GLASGOW | 19-20 May 2018

A celebration of the growing speciality coffee culture in Scotland with a two-day event showcasing the passion for quality coffee in our Scottish coffee community.

The festival will feature a multitude of coffee contributors, exhibitors, masterclasses, workshops, presentations and demonstrations.

**PLUS:** The event will be hosting the SCA UK Brewers Cup final

The Briggait | 141 Bridgegate | Glasgow | G1 5HZ

**f** GlasgowCoffeeFestival **🐦** glascoffeefest **📷** Glasgowcoffeefestival

# ᴹᴬᴾ№26. ALL THAT IS COFFEE

60-64 Osborne Street, Glasgow, G1 5QH

Palate-slappingly fresh coffee comes as standard at South Block's artisan espresso bar, as the top-grade beans filling the grinder are roasted just down the road at Dear Green.

The Glasgow roaster supplies this busy hub, in the belly of Merchant City's creative studios, with a weekly guest espresso as well as a killer house blend. Sample the latest batch on espresso or hit the retail haul and road test a new fave at home.

### INSIDER'S TIP THE GUYS HAVE SWAPPED SOY FOR BARISTA STANDARD OAT MILK THIS YEAR

The quality coffee is kept company by a mean selection of loose-leaf teas, locally baked cakes and simple lunches; pull up a chair in the bright space and sup in store or take along a KeepCup for your brew to-go.

And alongside regularly changing flavour profiles in each cup, you'll also find inspiration via the rotating exhibitions showcasing local artists and photographers. There's nothing like a dose of culture with your morning flattie to set you up for the day.

**ESTABLISHED**
2012

**KEY ROASTER**
Dear Green
Coffee Roasters

**BREWING METHOD**
Espresso

**MACHINE**
La Marzocco
Linea

**GRINDER**
Mazzer,
Mahlkonig
Tanzania

**OPENING HOURS**
**Mon-Fri**
8.45am-5pm

 Gluten FREE

 BEANS AVAILABLE / INSTORE

 ALTERNATIVE MILK

 WIFI

 CYCLE FRIENDLY

 DISABLED ACCESS

 BRING YOUR OWN Cup

T: 01412 714777
f All That is Coffee  @allthatis_coffee

# №27. THE GOOD COFFEE CARTEL

12 Cornwall Street, Kinning Park, Glasgow, G41 1AQ

Having learnt to roast, brew and serve top-grade beans at two of Glasgow's pioneering speciality pushers, Todd and Courtney – the coffee dealing duo behind the city's freshest roasting outfit – are shaking up the scene with their first solo venture.

It's a straight-up coffee situation at The Good Coffee Cartel. No tea, no hot chocolate and no brunch plates: just expertly-pulled espresso courtesy of the slick Kees van der Westen machine, fine filters on the hand brew bar and a solid offering via batch brew.

### INSIDER'S TIP CUDDLES WITH 'GUARD DOG' LUNA ARE AS ADDICTIVE AS THE BREWS

A set-up like this calls for beans of note. Happily, Courtney is doing the honours on a restored 1962 Probat UG15 (watch the roasting in action at the back of the shop) which stocks the cafe – along with a lengthy list of local coffee shops.

As one of the first spaces in Scotland to introduce a slot roasting system (which sells slots of time on the roaster), The Cartel enables home enthusiasts, local cafes and indie retailers to get in on the action and roast their own single origin beans, too.

**ESTABLISHED**
2017

**KEY ROASTER**
The Good
Coffee Cartel

**BREWING METHOD**
Espresso,
batch brew,
Chemex,
AeroPress,
Kinto range

**MACHINE**
Kees van der
Westen Mirage

**GRINDER**
Mythos One,
Mahlkonig EK 43

**OPENING HOURS**
**Mon-Sat**
9am-5pm

BEANS AVAILABLE
INSTORE

WiFi

CYCLE FRIENDLY

OUTDOOR seating

COFFEE COURSES

f The Good Coffee Cartel   🐦 @gdcoffeecartel   ◎ @thegoodcoffeecartel

# MAP 28. IT ALL STARTED HERE

75 Deanston Drive, Glasgow, G41 3AQ

After two years of pop-up caffeine hits at boutiques, bakeries, beer festivals and even a Sikh temple, It All Started Here has settled south side, bringing its brilliant brews to a permanent home in Shawlands.

It all started with coffee, and the team take it pretty seriously at this unique cafe and shop. Founder William Heenan is passionate about uncovering excellent beans, expanding the speciality palate and offering exciting experiences for coffee lovers – both the speciality savvy and coffee freshers. Those less familiar with quality caffeine can get their head around the basics at one of the regular cupping events.

### INSIDER'S TIP AN EXTENDED FOODIE OFFERING AND LONGER OPENING HOURS ARE IN THE PIPELINE

The weekly rotating coffee offering (prepared as espresso or batch brew) means visitors are introduced to a seasonal array of beans. Roasters from across the UK and Europe feature on the impressive bill – recent favourites have included big, bold naturals from Foundry, Crankhouse and Gardelli.

Look out for some fruity numbers pulled through the Aurelia in espresso based drinks. There's also a drool-worthy line-up of homemade bakes to sample.

**ESTABLISHED**
2017

**KEY ROASTER**
Multiple roasters

**BREWING METHOD**
Espresso, batch brew

**MACHINE**
Nuova Simonelli Aurelia (WBC spec)

**GRINDER**
Anfim SP-II, Mahlkonig Guatemala

**OPENING HOURS**
**Fri** 8am-3pm
**Sat-Sun**
9am-5pm

*Gluten* FREE

BEANS AVAILABLE
INSTORE

ALTE RNA TIVE MILK

WIFI

OUTDOOR SEATING

DISABLED ACCESS

COFFEE COURSES

---

www.allstartedhere.wordpress.com    T: 07743 069632

f It All Started Here   🐦 @allstartedhere   📷 @allstartedherecoffee

# Area 2

## ROASTERS & TRAINING

34 OVENBIRD COFFEE ROASTERS

# MAP 29. HOME GROUND COFFEE

Lyleston West Lodge, Cardross, Dumbarton, Argyll and Bute, G82 5HF

**A**lastair Moodie has come a long way since he started roasting in an old telephone exchange nine years ago.

From those humble beginnings, Home Ground has gone on to create bespoke blends for cafes, restaurants and hotels across the UK, clocking up prestigious milestones along the way.

The roastery was the first to serve cold brew at Latitude Festival and has supplied coffee to the Commonwealth Games. Alastair and team can also be found bringing cold brew and pourover refreshment to music, comedy and sport fans at events like T in the Park, Edinburgh Fringe and the Inveraray Games.

## LOOK OUT FOR DRAYMANS DARKSIDE – A COFFEE STOUT COLLABORATION WITH LOCAL BREWERY FYNE ALES

Training is a big priority and Alastair likes to ensure Home Ground customers are confident about brewing and serving single origins and carefully balanced blends to a top-notch standard.

Ethics are also high on the agenda: farmers receive a fair price for their beans, farming methods are sustainable and only traceable coffees make the cut.

ESTABLISHED
2008

ROASTER
MAKE & SIZE
Probat 5kg

OPEN
BY APPOINTMENT

COFFEE
COURSES

CUPPING
EVENTS

BEANS
AVAILABLE
ONLINE

www.homegroundcoffee.co.uk   T: 01389 841730

f Home Ground coffee shop   🐦 @the_coffee_guy   📷 @homeground.coffee

# 30. PAPERCUP COFFEE ROASTERS

12 Belmont Lane, Glasgow, G12 8EN

A short saunter from the Papercup cafe in Glasgow's West End is its new roastery – a restful refuge for those wishing to escape the hurly-burly of Great Western Road.

Coffee aficionados can visit the chilled industrial-chic space and relax with a coffee while watching the roast alchemy unfold.

**ESTABLISHED**
2015

**ROASTER**
**MAKE & SIZE**
Toper 3kg

**CAFE** ONSITE

**OPEN** TO THE PUBLIC

**COFFEE** COURSES

**BEANS** AVAILABLE
ONLINE ONSITE

## 'THE GANG ENJOY NOTHING MORE THAN A GOOD CHAT ABOUT THE BREW'

All of the roasting action for Papercup's cafes, wholesale partners and home brewing fans goes down here, as the team carefully roast small lots of high scoring coffees which are exclusively sourced via direct trade agreements.

The gang enjoy nothing more than a good chat about the brew while the intense aroma of browning beans awakens the senses. And if that doesn't trigger the endorphins, the taste of an exquisite coffee and wedge of homemade banana bread from the bar should do the trick.

Tasting the fruits of the roasting team's labours is just one of the perks of visiting the Belmont Lane roastery: cuppings, training nights and pop-up art and craft events also take place regularly.

**www.papercupcoffee.co.uk**   T: 07456 487226
f Papercup Coffee Company   🐦 @pccoffeeuk   📷 @pccoffeeuk

# N.º 31. THE STEAMIE COFFEE ROASTERS

1024 Argyle Street, Glasgow, G3 8LX

The Steamie only started roasting the speciality coffee served at its Finnieston cafe in 2016, yet this year the team are already planning to move to a more spacious venue to craft their small batch, single origin beans.

Roaster and barista Luc currently stocks the coffee shop's grinders and impressive retail selection from a 5kg Has Garanti drum roaster, working with owner Stephen to ethically source green beans that provide a positive social impact throughout the coffee chain.

'We are immensely proud to be a small batch roaster,' says Stephen. 'We only buy exclusive micro lots, competition and Cup of Excellence coffees which allow us to offer unique profiles.'

## THERE ARE PLANS FOR DEDICATED SENSORY AND CUPPING ROOMS AS WELL AS A LAB AT THE NEW VENUE

The line-up changes according to the coffee seasons, with an atlas-worth of regional varieties to explore at the cafe or from The Steamie's webstore. 'We follow the harvest around the world to ensure our beans are always at optimum flavour potential,' adds Stephen.

**ESTABLISHED**
2016

**ROASTER**
MAKE & SIZE
Has Garanti
HSR5 5kg

CAFE
ONSITE

OPEN
BY APPOINTMENT

COFFEE
COURSES

BEANS
AVAILABLE
ONLINE    ONSITE

**www.thesteamie.co.uk**   T: 07821 544449

f The Steamie Coffee Roasters   🐦 @the_steamie   📷 @thesteamie

# MAP Nº32. DEAR GREEN COFFEE ROASTERS

Unit 2, 13-27 East Campbell Street, Glasgow, G1 5DT

Founded in 2011 by Lisa Lawson, Dear Green has been instrumental in driving forward speciality in Scotland. And, passionate about the whole coffee process, the Glasgow roastery has always been steered by its ethical and social conscience.

There's a bond of trust between Dear Green and its traders and growers, and the team make sure to go to origin every year. The resulting strong relationships bore fruit in the form of Dear Green's first direct trade coffee this year.

Beans generally come from South America and Africa, though the key to everything sourced is *'quality flavour notes and seasonality,'* says Lisa.

The social conscience comes into play at home too, with Dear Green often raising money for charity through innovative ideas such as selling coffee sacks for upcycling.

## LOOK OUT FOR ROASTING CLASSES COMING SOON

As well as setting up the roastery, Lisa is responsible for the Glasgow Coffee Festival and the Scottish AeroPress Championship and is a qualified SCA trainer who offers courses in sensory skills and barista training.

**ESTABLISHED**
2011

**ROASTER**
MAKE & SIZE
Probat P25 25kg
Probat L12 12kg
1 barrel sample
roaster 100g
IKAWA 80g

OPEN
BY APPOINTMENT

COFFEE COURSES

COURSES

BEANS
AVAILABLE
ONLINE

www.deargreencoffee.com  T: 01415 527774
f Dear Green Coffee Roasters  🐦 @coffeeglasgow  📷 @deargreen

# MAP 33. DEAR GREEN COFFEE SCHOOL

Unit 2, 13-27 East Campbell Street, Glasgow, G1 5DT

This is the only roastery in Scotland where you can take SCA approved sensory and barista courses. And, since opening in 2011, Dear Green has been a guiding light for many a pro barista.

The East Campbell Street roastery has always made a point of offering free barista training for wholesale customers, but there are now options for all levels of coffee experience, starting with the two hour coffee brew class. Soak up specialist advice on how to brew like a pro at home and you'll also learn more detailed aspects such as which coffee and brew styles suit individual tastes.

For the geeks there's an espresso masterclass, aimed at creating a new level of skilled barista. It gives beginners all the basics on how to master the equipment, right through to the intricacies of fourth-wave espresso extraction yield analysis.

**ESTABLISHED**
2011

OPEN
BY APPOINTMENT

COFFEE
COURSES

COURSES

BEANS
AVAILABLE

ONLINE

## 'FOR THE GEEKS THERE'S AN ESPRESSO MASTERCLASS, AIMED AT CREATING A NEW LEVEL OF SKILLED BARISTA'

As part of the Roaster Guild of Europe, SCA-authorised trainer/owner Lisa Lawson is at the forefront of advancements in the roasting community and is constantly adapting and improving her Glasgow roastery.

**www.deargreencoffee.com** T: 01415 527774

f Dear Green Coffee Roasters  🐦 @coffeeglasgow  📷 @deargreen

# 34. OVENBIRD COFFEE ROASTERS

Unit 3, Clifford Court, 179 Woodville Street, Glasgow, G51 2RQ

S uch was the success of Ovenbird's whisky barrel-aged beans that the Glasgow roaster introduced three more coffees to its boozy collection this year.

Maturing green beans in emptied barrels for 12, 18 and 21 weeks, owner Davide Angeletti has created a marriage of coffee and whisky which packs just the right punch for a post-supper espresso or affogato.

**ESTABLISHED**
2013

**ROASTER**
MAKE & SIZE
R&R 15kg

**COFFEE COURSES**

**BEANS AVAILABLE**
ONLINE  ONSITE

## 'WE'RE SOURCING COFFEE FROM SAKE WOMEN'S ALLIANCE IN RWANDA'

It's not just the retail collection that has expanded either. The roastery recently moved to larger premises to make room for a fresh cafe set-up, and traded in the old roaster for a 15kg batch R&R. If that wasn't enough, the team have committed even more time to developing direct trade relationships with coffee farmers in Africa.

'We're sourcing coffee from a number of certified farms including Sake Women's Alliance in Rwanda,' explains Davide. 'This new washing station gives women more ownership within the coffee industry, and the fully-washed beans they're producing create a well-balanced cup with orange peel and tangy citrus overtones.'

Other coffees on the bill for the popular subscription service include the chocolatey Dead Poets Society, fruity Nineteen Eighty-Four and the 'not bad for a decaf' water-processed Mexico La Laja.

**www.ovenbird.co.uk**  T: 01414 453200

f Ovenbird Coffee Roasters   @ovenbird_coffee   @ovenbird_coffee

# MAP 35. THOMSON'S COFFEE ROASTERS

Burnfield Avenue, Thornliebank, Glasgow, G46 7TL

Thomson's couldn't be prouder to be an independently owned Scottish family business with 176 years of heritage to draw upon.

Its history entails many pioneering acts (David Thomson opened Scotland's first speciality coffee shop in 1841) and fascinating firsts (its Napier Coffee Apparatus was a forerunner to the syphon). The innovation continues with the new roastery, cafe, training centre and events space in Glasgow city centre that's due to open in early 2018.

## ROASTING TAKES PLACE ON BOTH A 1940S WHITMEE AND SCOTLAND'S FIRST LORING KESTREL

*'It's good to have a presence in Glasgow where the business was founded,'* says managing director Russell Jenkins. *'As the oldest speciality coffee business in Glasgow, we wanted to have a dedicated space where people can see what we're doing, try the coffee and check out our training space which will support the coffee community.'*

The new roastery, underneath Glasgow Central station, is another milestone for a company that puts quality and integrity at the heart of everything it does: from roasting blends with provenance to sourcing single origins and exclusive micro lots.

**ESTABLISHED**
1841

**ROASTER**
MAKE & SIZE
Loring Kestrel 35kg
Whitmee Direct Flame 35kg

CAFE ONSITE

OPEN BY APPOINTMENT

COFFEE COURSES

COURSES

BEANS AVAILABLE
ONLINE  ONSITE

www.thomsonscoffee.com   T: 01416 370683

f Thomsons Coffee   🐦 @thomsonscoffee   📷 @thomsonscoffee

## CAFE

36 Habitat Cafe
37 The Bach
38 Pacamara Food & Drink
39 Zest Cafe
40 Fallen Tree Coffee Truck
41 Sable & Flea
42 Coffee on Wooer

## ROASTER

43 Glen Lyon Coffee Roasters
44 Sacred Grounds Coffee Company
45 The Bean Shop
46 Unorthodox Roasters

All locations are approximate

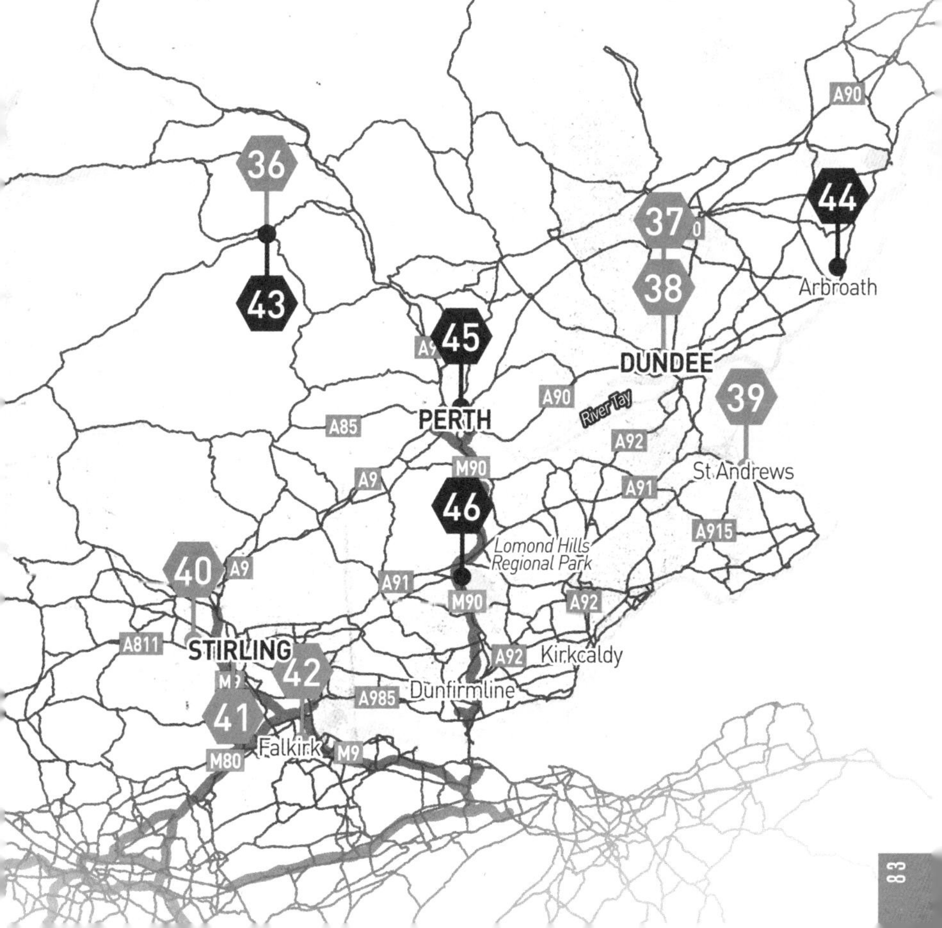

A90
36
44
37
38
43
Arbroath
45
DUNDEE
39
A90
River Tay
PERTH
A85
A92
M90
St Andrews
A9
A91
46
A915
Lomond Hills
Regional Park
40
A9
A91
M90
A92
A811
STIRLING
42
A92
Kirkcaldy
A985
Dunfermline
41
Falkirk
M9
M80

# MAP№36. HABITAT CAFE

1 The Square, Aberfeldy, Perthshire, PH15 2DD

There are secret signs that caffeine buffs look for to identify cafes that are likely to serve a decent brew: a blackboard detailing the day's coffees, equipment to buy for the amateur brew bar, and beans available to take home being just a few ...

But even with those boxes ticked, visitors to Habitat are always surprised to find a coffee shop of such rare note in this small rural town.

Owner and barista-in-chief, Mike Haggerton, seems to rather enjoy surpassing visitors' expectations. And there's no doubt that he does: the full monty of serve styles are employed to produce the elixir extracted from the Has Bean crop.

## INSIDER'S TIP GET YOURSELF ON ONE OF MIKE'S IN-HOUSE COFFEE COURSES

It's also worth asking if there are any secret coffee options available 'under the counter', as they often have small amounts of other good finds that they're happy to share with bean brethren.

Serving craft beers is this year's new development, and you'll find as much focus on tea as coffee – Habitat was the national winner of the Tea Accolade from the Beverage Standards Association in 2016.

**ESTABLISHED**
2012

**KEY ROASTER**
Has Bean Coffee

**BREWING METHOD**
Espresso,
Kalita Wave,
AeroPress,
Clever Dripper,
syphon,
woodneck,
Chemex, V60

**MACHINE**
Nuova Simonelli
Aurelia II T3

**GRINDER**
Mahlkonig,
Compak

**OPENING HOURS**
Seasonal
opening hours

---

**www.habitatcafe.co.uk**  T: 01887 822944

f Habitat Cafe   🐦 @habitatcafe   📷 @habitatcafeaberfeldy

# ᴹᴬᴾ**37. THE BACH**

31 Albert Square, Dundee, Tayside, DD1 1DJ

After a morning at Dundee's McManus art gallery and museum, culture vultures can now refresh for the afternoon by sinking their talons into a well-crafted speciality coffee at The Bach.

The Kiwi-style cafe has upped sticks and set up across the road from the gallery and offers a menu of cosmopolitan brekkie, brunch and lunch dishes. Expect a mash-up of cool Kiwiana, Mediterranean and Asian-influenced food and Scottish staples.

Everything is made in house including burger patties, sausages, beans and granola – even the habanero ketchup and chilli jam are rustled up on the premises.

### INSIDER'S TIP SOFT BREW? TRY IT IN FIVE WAYS AT THE BACH

It's not just the Kiwi burgers and mince on toast that customers flock for, of course. The coffee – courtesy of local roaster Sacred Grounds is a big draw, and pairs perfectly with the eye-popping pageant of Bach-made cakes, slices and biscuits.

And don't leave without appeasing your inner six-year-old with Kiwi lollies such as Jaffas, Peanut Slabs, Pineapple Lumps and Tim Tams.

ESTABLISHED
2016

KEY ROASTER
Sacred Grounds Coffee Company

BREWING METHOD
Espresso, V60, AeroPress, Chemex, syphon, french press

MACHINE
Rocket Espresso RES

GRINDER
Fiorenzato

OPENING HOURS
**Mon-Sun**
9am-5pm

**www.the-bach.com**   T: 01382 869902
f The Bach  @thebachbistro

# MAP № 38. PACAMARA FOOD & DRINK

302 Perth Road, Dundee, DD2 1AU

**D**undee's first speciality shop is celebrating its fifth birthday this year. For half a decade, Pacamara (formerly Espress Oh!) has put Dundee on the map for bangin' brekkies and stonking speciality.

Make sure to rock up at this friendly, vintage-style coffee shop early: Pacamara has been gently flexing its culinary muscles and the word is out. As well as first-rate coffee, its simple and tasty brunch menu makes it one of the city's best breakfast joints.

Pillowy scrambled eggs, fennel sausage patty, crispy halloumi, beer baked beans and housemade hash browns are just some of the get-out-of-bed incentives on the menu. Although if you miss the early shift there's always a lunchtime line-up of handmade burgers and brunch dishes served until late afternoon.

## INSIDER'S TIP
### REGULARS RAVE ABOUT THE HOUSE HASH BROWNS

The Has Bean house blend for milk based drinks is complemented by a rotating guest espresso for aficionados after something more adventurous. You'll also find two additional filter options on the go and bags of beans and brewing equipment to take home.

**ESTABLISHED**
2013

**KEY ROASTER**
Has Bean Coffee

**BREWING METHOD**
Espresso,
AeroPress,
pourover

**MACHINE**
Victoria Arduino
Black Eagle

**GRINDER**
Mahlkonig K30,
Mahlkonig EK 43
Mythos One

**OPENING HOURS**
**Mon–Fri** 9am-5pm
**Sat** 9.30am-5pm
**Sun** 9.30am-4pm

Gluten FREE

BEANS AVAILABLE INSTORE

ALTERNATIVE MILK

OUTDOOR seating

FAMILY FRIENDLY

DISABLED ACCESS

**www.pacamara.co.uk**   T: 01382 527666
f Pacamara Food & Drink   @ @pacamaradundee

# 39. ZEST CAFE

95 South Street, St Andrews, Fife, KY16 9QW

With a passion for inspiring people and communities, as well as creating top-notch food and drink, this unique cafe lives up to its name.

Zest's owner, Lisa Cathro, has created a business which values its staff as much as its customers. She's dedicated to training her team and, since opening a decade ago, has won countless awards for her work.

### INSIDER'S TIP: ENJOY AN ALFRESCO LUNCH – ZEST IS ON THE SUNNY SIDE OF THE STREET

Staff receive the very best barista coaching, and Lisa goes the extra mile in terms of employing and developing the skills of people with disabilities, mental health issues and those facing barriers to employment.

Lisa's own coffee skills are second to none: she's an SCA AST authorised trainer and runs courses at Thomson's Coffee Roasters in Glasgow. She's even used her skills to develop a barista training programme for prisoners, a scheme run with hospitality charity Springboard UK.

With all the great work going down at Zest, we reckon the team deserve the occasional time-out to revel in one of their Glen Lyon espressos – with a topped waffle or packed-full-of-goodies bagel on the side.

**ESTABLISHED**
2008

**KEY ROASTER**
Glen Lyon
Coffee Roasters

**BREWING METHOD**
Espresso, V60,
drip filter,
cold brew

**MACHINE**
Victoria Arduino
Black Eagle

**GRINDER**
Mahlkonig K30,
Mahlkonig Vario,
Mazzer Luigi
Major, Ceado E7

**OPENING HOURS**
**Mon-Sun**
8am-6pm
(seasonal
opening hours)

 Gluten FREE

 BEANS AVAILABLE INSTORE

 ALTERNATIVE MILK

 WIFI

 CYCLE FRIENDLY

 OUTDOOR seating

 FAMILY friendly

 DISABLED ACCESS

 BRING YOUR OWN Cup

 COFFEE COURSES

www.**wearezest**.co.uk   T: 01334 471451
f Zest Cafe  @ @zeststandrews

# MAP № 40. FALLEN TREE COFFEE TRUCK

Blair Drummond, near Stirling

'**N**o event is too rural or muddy: we love the challenge,' declares the owner of this Land Rover Defender-turned-coffee shop on wheels.

Former city barista Michelle Kibaris decided there was no reason why people shouldn't enjoy a speciality brew wherever they happened to be – even in the wilds of the Scottish landscape – so went mobile in October 2016.

Cleverly adapting the vehicle to house a generator and the all-important Linea Mini machine, Michelle's Fallen Tree Coffee Truck can be found at events across central Scotland.

### INSIDER'S TIP TRY AN ICED CAPPUCCINO – IT LOOKS AND TASTES AMAZING

Switching up the roasts as regularly as the venue, the Mythos One grinder has welcomed Curve, Round Hill, Papercup and Dear Green beans, and alongside the espresso based drinks there's also batch brew available. For summer sipping, try a fruity cold brew, while winter specials such as the homemade chai lattes are particularly toothsome.

Another quirky addition is the vintage orange juicer: mesmerising – and a hit with kids and grown-ups.

**ESTABLISHED**
2016

**KEY ROASTER**
Multiple roasters

**BREWING METHOD**
Espresso, batch brew, cold brew

**MACHINE**
La Marzocco Linea Mini

**GRINDER**
Mythos One

**OPENING HOURS**
As per event

Gluten FREE

ALTERNATIVE MILK

OUTDOOR Seating

BRING YOUR OWN Cup

---

**www.fallentreeworkshop.com/coffeetruck**   T: 07415 491195

f Fallen Tree Coffee Truck   @fallentreecoffeetruck

# №41. SABLE & FLEA

12 Friars Street, Stirling, FK8 1HA

There aren't many coffee shops in the world – let alone in Scotland – where you can buy a stuffed bird with your latte.

Sable & Flea is unique by any standards: call in for a coffee and you'll find yourself amid a host of quirky and unusual household items (including the taxidermy).

## INSIDER'S TIP BRING THE POOCH ALONG FOR YOUR TOASTED CHOCOLATE BUN FIX

Owner Suzi Carr spent over two decades in Melbourne (hence her love of speciality coffee) and has combined a passion for the bean with her skills as an interior designer to create a unique cafe/homeware hybrid.

It's a bit tucked away so look for the green, old fashioned shop front. And once inside you'll be drawn to linger – thanks to the friendly staff, great coffee and healthy homemade food. We'd also recommend indulging in a slice of the almond pistachio and white chocolate cake.

With its Nude house roast, the tiled coffee bar is the focal point downstairs – or slip into the sunny courtyard for summer sipping. Then, suitably buzzing, head upstairs to explore the treasure trove of vintage and designer homewares.

**ESTABLISHED**
2015

**KEY ROASTER**
Nude Coffee Roasters

**BREWING METHOD**
Espresso, V60

**MACHINE**
La Marzocco Linea Classic

**GRINDER**
Mazzer Major

**OPENING HOURS**
**Tue-Fri**
10am-5pm
**Sat**
9.30am-5.30pm

 Gluten FREE

 BEANS AVAILABLE INSTORE

 ALTERNATIVE MILK

 WIFI

 CYCLE FRIENDLY

 OUTDOOR SEATING

 FAMILY FRIENDLY

DISABLED ACCESS

**www.sableandflea.com** T: 01786 475597

f Sable and Flea  @sableflea

# 42. COFFEE ON WOOER

2-4 Wooer Street, Falkirk, Stirlingshire, FK1 1NJ

S etting the standard for speciality in Stirlingshire is the award winning Coffee on Wooer (CoW to regulars).

Getting Falkirk folk excited about a carefully crafted cup, the team's artisan approach is inspired by the building's history – it once housed a drapery. Homage is paid to this in the retro interior and walls pasted with original Victorian invoices.

### INSIDER'S TIP BEAN LOVERS (OF THE FOODIE VARIETY) CAN JOIN CoW'S VEGAN CLUB, THE TARTAN CARROT

It's all about the coffee at CoW. *'I regularly travel to America and always bring back a couple of bags for the hopper,'* explains owner Rory. *'We've had coffee from Dubai and from a variety of American states over the years.'*

Aside from the transatlantic trips, keeping it local is high on the agenda. The exclusive house espresso from Thomson's in Glasgow sits beside a growing gang of guest espressos from regional roasters, pulled through the snazzy new Victoria Arduino Gravitech.

And having palled up with local butchers, bakers and delis, most of what's on your plate can be traced to within four miles of the shop. That's how we like it.

**ESTABLISHED**
2013

**KEY ROASTER**
Thomson's
Coffee Roasters

**BREWING METHOD**
Espresso,
AeroPress

**MACHINE**
Victoria Arduino
Black Eagle
Gravitech

**GRINDER**
Victoria Arduino
Mythos One,
Mazzer Luigi

**OPENING HOURS**
**Mon-Thu**
8.30am-5pm
**Fri-Sat**
8.30am-7.30pm
**Sun** 10am-5pm

 Gluten FREE

 BEANS AVAILABLE EN STORE

 ALTERNATIVE MILK

 WIFI

 CYCLE FRIENDLY

 OUTDOOR seating

 FAMILY FRIENDLY

 DISABLED ACCESS

www.coffeeonwooer.co.uk   T: 01324 278026

f Coffee On Wooer   🐦 @cowfalkirk   📷 @cowfalkirk

Amew 3
ROASTERS

# MAP 43. GLEN LYON COFFEE ROASTERS

Aberfeldy Business Park, Dunkeld Road, Aberfeldy, Perthshire, PH15 2AQ

**N**ature, travel and adventure: these are the themes which not only characterise the spirit of Glen Lyon but also the quest for coffee perfection. Fitting, then, that this small batch roaster was 'born' on the top of a mountain.

*'We started roasting coffee in our bothy in Glen Lyon back in 2011,'* says owner Fiona Grant, who runs the business with husband Jamie. *'After several winters spent digging lorry deliveries out of snowdrifts, we moved the roastery to Aberfeldy, a cool little town on the banks of the River Tay.'*

When they're not roasting, the Glen Lyon team of five are out exploring the surrounding landscape or travelling the world, searching for exceptional beans. Traceability is important to Fiona who can usually name the farmer who grew every coffee they sell.

## 'TRAVELLING THE WORLD, SEARCHING FOR EXCEPTIONAL BEANS'

Working with around 12 countries, they buy seasonally, sourcing speciality, often organic, hand-picked beans. Last year they journeyed to Antioquia in Colombia and Bolivia on the bean trail. They've also hosted return visits, including one from Diego Robelo of Aquiares Estate, Costa Rica's first carbon neutral coffee farm.

**ESTABLISHED**
2011

**ROASTER**
MAKE & SIZE
Probat 12kg

OPEN
TO THE PUBLIC

COFFEE
COURSES

BEANS
AVAILABLE
ONLINE ONSITE

www.glenlyoncoffee.co.uk  T: 01887 822817
f Glen Lyon Coffee  🐦 @glenlyoncoffee  📷 @glenlyoncoffee

# 44. SACRED GROUNDS COFFEE COMPANY

Unit 15, Arbroath Business Centre, 31 Dens Road, Arbroath, Angus, DD11 1RS

**A**rbroath may be famed for one particular foodie phenomenon, but another artisan producer is lining up to take its place alongside the haddock smokie.

Sacred Grounds was set up by brother and sister Ian and Kathryn Baker with long-term friend Jamie Simpson. As the only roastery in Angus, the trio are taking seriously their responsibility of providing the area with a supply of expertly roasted beans. *'We want to educate, inspire and enthuse the people of Angus and beyond,'* says Kathryn.

Their task is made easier by their pride and joy, a 5kg Toper roaster called Fatima.

**ESTABLISHED**
2015

**ROASTER**
MAKE & SIZE
Toper 5kg

OPEN
BY APPOINTMENT

BEANS
AVAILABLE
ONLINE

## 'ANOTHER ARTISAN PRODUCER IS LINING UP TO TAKE ITS PLACE ALONGSIDE THE HADDOCK SMOKIE'

*'She's a valued member of the team, with a long history of producing the finest coffees in the Scottish roasting community,'* adds Kathryn. It seems that every coffee geek in the land knows Fatima and, in a happy twist of fate, she was the very machine on which chief roaster Jamie learned his craft, many years ago.

The team are meticulous in their sourcing of ethically produced green beans. The roasted versions are available online, although it's a whole bean-only situation as the guys insist on grinding to-demand to ensure maximum quality – it is 'sacred' after all …

**www.sacred-grounds.coffee**  T: 07808 806610

Sacred Grounds Coffee Company  @sacredgrounds14  @sacred_grounds_coffee_company

# 45. THE BEAN SHOP

67 George Street, Perth, Perthshire, PH1 5LB

It's all in the detail at The Bean Shop in Perth. Little touches mark this roastery out as special: those who swing by get a free sample of the coffee of the month while a little choccie is popped into every box of beans posted out to the band of subscribers.

A real desire to delight and please is at the heart of this chatty team led by husband and wife John and Lorna Bruce. Whatever sustainable, ethical coffee you desire, the family roastery comes up with the goods: Fairtrade, organic, Rainforest Alliance, swiss water decaffeinated, geisha, maragogype, peaberry or natural process. And a new eco-friendly Loring roaster provides an innovative, clean and efficient yield.

**ESTABLISHED**
2003

**ROASTER**
MAKE & SIZE
Sivetz 17kg
Loring 15kg
Probat 5kg

BEANS AVAILABLE
ONLINE ONSITE

## 'A CHOCCIE IS POPPED INTO EVERY BOX OF BEANS POSTED'

This same caring approach is taken in the sourcing of the green beans, and the roastery has nurtured relationships with farming families in Honduras, Peru and Colombia, buying from them each year to provide a stable and reliable income.

Visitors can drop by and sample the latest espresso – be sure to take a large shopper so you can stock up on the latest brewing gear, ceramics and speciality teas.

**www.thebeanshop.co.uk**   T: 01738 449955
f The Bean Shop   🐦 @thebeanshopuk   📷 @thebeanshopuk

NO 1
PEEBLES ROAD

# MAP 46. UNORTHODOX ROASTERS

129 High Street, Kinross, KY13 8AQ

**A**fter 10 months spent border-hopping across Latin America, roasting coffee metamorphosed from a pipe dream to reality for entrepreneurial mates Neil Buchan and Christopher Bode.

The journey continued with experiments in the frying pan, though fast forward a few months and the sustainably sourced green beans were – and still are – being given the small batch treatment in a nifty 6kg Giesen.

Having moved from caffeine super-fans to pro roasters, the Unorthodox chaps are keen to help newbies recreate the speciality experience at home and are always up for a quick grilling or impromptu demo.

Catch them at their in-house cafe, where a custom built copper brew bar houses eight V60s. We'd recommend imbibing a cafe au lait made with Wee Stoater beans for a lip-smacking caramel hit.

## THE UNORTHODOX GUYS ARE BUSY CREATING A 'REVOLUTIONARY HOT CHOC' ... EXPECT A FLAVOUR REVELATION

Keen to challenge perceptions of what coffee should be, Neil and Christopher are boldly calling out filter as the new espresso. Order coffee to be delivered to your door or sample at UDX HQ and see if you concur.

**ESTABLISHED**
2016

**ROASTER**
MAKE & SIZE
Giesen
W6A 6kg

CAFE ONSITE

OPEN BY APPOINTMENT

BEANS AVAILABLE
ONLINE / CAFES ETC

---

www.unorthodoxroasters.co.uk   T: 07834 955301

 Unorthodox Roasters   🐦 @unorthodoxroast   📷 @unorthodoxroasters

55 CAIRNGORM
COFFEE

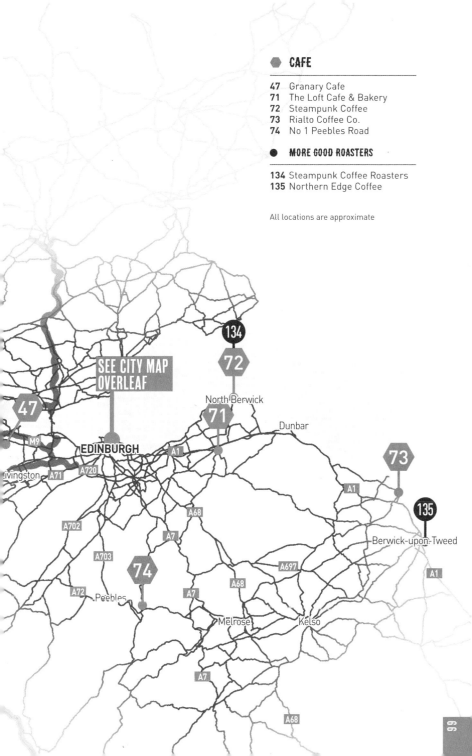

## ⬡ CAFE

**47** Granary Cafe
**71** The Loft Cafe & Bakery
**72** Steampunk Coffee
**73** Rialto Coffee Co.
**74** No 1 Peebles Road

## ● MORE GOOD ROASTERS

**134** Steampunk Coffee Roasters
**135** Northern Edge Coffee

All locations are approximate

**SEE CITY MAP OVERLEAF**

North Berwick

Dunbar

EDINBURGH

Livingston

Berwick-upon-Tweed

Peebles

Melrose

Kelso

All locations are approximate

SEE FULL LOCATION
DETAILS OVERLEAF

A199

124

123

PORTOBELLO

Holyrood Park

Arthur's Seat

133

77

NIDDRIE

## ⬡ CAFE

## ⬡ ROASTER

## ⬡ TRAINING

## MORE GOOD CUPS

## MORE GOOD ROASTERS

# №47. GRANARY CAFE

102 High Street, Linlithgow, West Lothian, EH49 7AQ

'I'm a food enthusiast – and I blame my grandmother,' smiles Gillian Fraser, owner of new neighbourhood nook, Granary Cafe.

Training in the world of incredible edibles started early for Gillian. From weighing out dried fruit and coffee beans, to pricing products and serving customers at her gran's health food shop, a passion for wholesome, nutritious fare was ingrained early. Gran's shop was even called The Granary, providing inspiration for the name of Gillian's West Lothian cafe.

### INSIDER'S TIP BRING YOUR FOUR-LEGGED PAL ALONG: GRANARY IS A POOCH-FRIENDLY SPOT

The seed continued to grow and, after years working with some of Scotland's top chefs and professionals in the hospitality arena, Gillian decided to leave the corporate world in favour of a new venture: cultivating a haven of wholesome food and cracking espressos for the folk of Linlithgow.

Beans come from Aberfeldy friends, Glen Lyon, and the current fave, Red Stag, fills the hopper. Pulled through the Esprezzi machine, it's a bold and fruity Latin American/East African blend with a lingering chocolatey finish.

**ESTABLISHED**
2017

**KEY ROASTER**
Glen Lyon
Coffee Roasters

**BREWING METHOD**
Espresso

**MACHINE**
Esprezzi

**GRINDER**
Fiorenzato F64E

**OPENING HOURS**
**Tue-Fri**
8am-4pm
**Sat** 8am-5pm
**Sun** 9am-4pm

 Gluten FREE

 BEANS AVAILABLE INSTORE

 ALTERNATIVE MILK

 WIFI

 OUTDOOR seating

---

**www.granary.scot**   T: 01506 253408

f Granary  @ @granarycafelinlithgow

# 48. FILAMENT COFFEE – EAST TRINITY ROAD

44a East Trinity Road, Edinburgh, EH5 3DJ

**S**ucker for the hiss of the steam wand, hum of buzzy chatter and sizzle of toasties on the grill? Give your sensory cafe experience a roaster upgrade with the waft of gently roasting beans and the mesmerising whirl of the drum at Filament's new venture.

Moving a Probatone 5 roaster into the East Trinity Road venue, the Filament fraternity are roasting, grinding, brewing and serving an exclusively single origin line-up of beans at the Scandi-cool set-up. *'We wanted to give our guests the chance to see the bean-to-cup process,'* enthuses manager Matej.

### INSIDER'S TIP SCORE ONE OF THE THREE TABLES ON THE MEZZANINE FLOOR

Creating a continental coffee house vibe in suburban Edinburgh, the guys have adopted table service for their menu of espresso based drinks, filter coffees and pared-back lunch plates. Secure a stool in the window or nab one of the contemporary tables and let the baristas talk you through the latest flavour profiles.

The offering may be specialist but this is a relaxed spot: meet friends, talk coffee, scoff cake and bring the pooch along to the party.

**ESTABLISHED**
2017

**KEY ROASTER**
Filament Coffee Roastery

**BREWING METHOD**
Espresso, V60

**MACHINE**
La Marzocco Linea

**GRINDER**
Mythos One, Mahlkonig Guatemala, Ceado

**OPENING HOURS**
**Mon-Fri**
8am-6pm
**Sat-Sun**
9am-6pm

 Gluten FREE

 BEANS AVAILABLE INSTORE

 ALTERNATIVE MILK

 WIFI

 CYCLE FRIENDLY

 FAMILY FRIENDLY

 DISABLED ACCESS

---

www.filamentcoffee.com   T: 07712 218884
f Filament Coffee   @ @filament_roastery

# MAP № 49. ARTISAN ROAST COFFEE ROASTERS – STOCKBRIDGE

100a Raeburn Place, Edinburgh, EH4 1HH

A tour of the original sparks which ignited the Scottish speciality explosion wouldn't be complete without hitting the clan of Artisan Roast cafes.

The Artisan story started in 2007 on Broughton Street, before a second cafe popped up in Bruntsfield, followed by a third on Gibson Street – its first Glaswegian venture. The Stockbridge outpost may be the baby of the bunch but, just like its sisters, it's fuelling a passion for great coffee in its neighbourhood.

## INSIDER'S TIP
### THIS IS A POPULAR HANGOUT FOR STOCKBRIDGE'S FOUR-LEGGED HOMIES TOO

Cross the wooden floors to the dashing brew bar to order beautiful breakfast and lunch dishes prepared with locally sourced ingredients, along with a carefully crafted coffee. Pass the shelves groaning with own-roasted beans on the way back to your perch and decide which of the single origin lovelies you'll take home later.

There's always a hefty seasonal selection to sample, as the gang have up to ten beans from around the world on the go at any time. If you forget to restock your stash in store, get your mitts on a bag or two online – where you can find videos to get a feel of Artisan's other cafes.

**ESTABLISHED**
2015

**KEY ROASTER**
Artisan Roast Coffee Roasters

**BREWING METHOD**
Espresso, V60, AeroPress, Chemex, syphon

**MACHINE**
La Marzocco Linea PB

**GRINDER**
Nuova Simonelli, Mazzer Major electronic

**OPENING HOURS**
**Mon-Fri**
8.30am-6pm
**Sat-Sun**
9.30am-5pm

 Gluten FREE

 BEANS AVAILABLE INSTORE

 ALTERNATIVE MILK

 WIFI

 CYCLE FRIENDLY

 OUTDOOR seating

 FAMILY friendly

 DISABLED ACCESS

 BRING YOUR OWN Cup

 COFFEE COURSES

www.artisanroast.co.uk   T: 01313 328834
f Artisan Roast _ Stockbridge   🐦 @artisanroast   📷 @artisanroastcoffeeroasters

# MAP№50. NO 33

33 Deanhaugh Street, Edinburgh, EH4 1LR

The coffee changes with the seasons at No 33, so there's always something exciting to explore.

The introduction of a Moccamaster this year is yet another draw for Edinburgh's bean geeks, who visit to sample interesting beans such as Hernado Chantre via batch brew or the nutty, floral, lychee-sweet Conception Pixcaya on espresso.

The cafe's street corner position and big picture windows make it stand out in one of the city's slickest neighbourhoods. Inside, it's airy and uncluttered with a great playlist completing the relaxed vibe.

If you're like us, once armed with a damn fine coffee from the bar you'll want to find a perch by the window and partake in a little sugary indulgence as you watch the world scurry by.

### INSIDER'S TIP KEEP AN EYE ON SOCIAL MEDIA FOR POP-UPS AND OFF-THE-CUFF EVENTS

The food offering is another lure: it's all homemade and ranges from smoked salmon-stuffed bagels to halloumi flatbread and chicken, bacon and guacamole focaccia. There are colourful bowls of soup, too, and word is that a new cake supplier has introduced a mean victoria sponge. Save us a slice.

**ESTABLISHED**
2014

**KEY ROASTER**
Williams & Johnson Coffee Co.

**BREWING METHOD**
Espresso, Moccamaster batch brew

**MACHINE**
Elektra

**GRINDER**
Mazzer

**OPENING HOURS**
**Mon-Fri**
8am-5pm
**Sat-Sun**
9am-5pm

www.thenewtowndeli.com    T: 01313 328353
@cafeno.33

# №51. LOVECRUMBS – STOCKBRIDGE
22 St Stephen Street, Edinburgh, EH3 5AL

L ovecrumbs' new little sister shop in Stockbridge is right at home among St Stephen Street's network of indie finds.

A pocket-sized version of the West Port venue, mini lovecrumbs only started slinging on-the-go 'spros in October 2017, but you'll already find quite a queue at the Rocket Boxer machine.

Spot the local coffee lovers emerging from the new hangout with a KeepCup in one hand and a box of LC signature bakes in the other and its popularity soon makes sense.

### INSIDER'S TIP  THE LOCAL LEGACY CONTINUES IN THE LATTES AS MOSSGIEL MILK IS LAVISHED ON ESPRESSO

Steampunk continues to supply North Berwick-roasted beans, while a team of bakers at HQ whip up the creative cake combos including blueberry and lemon, gooseberry and spelt, and apricot and lavender.

They've also teamed up with the guys at Century General Store, so don't leave without browsing the beautiful homewares, cards, stationery and design-led lovelies.

**ESTABLISHED**
2017

**KEY ROASTER**
Steampunk Coffee

**BREWING METHOD**
Espresso

**MACHINE**
Rocket Boxer

**GRINDER**
Anfim

**OPENING HOURS**
**Wed-Fri**
11am-6pm
**Sat-Sun**
10am-6pm

 BEANS AVAILABLE INSTORE

 ALTERNATIVE MILK

 WIFI

 FAMILY FRIENDLY

 BRING YOUR OWN CUP

www.lovecrumbs.co.uk

 f Lovecrumbs  🐦 @hellolovecrumbs  📷 @hellolovecrumbs

# №52. LEO'S BEANERY

23a Howe Street, Edinburgh, EH3 6TF

A head of the curve and serving speciality since 2009, Joe and Marie Denby run a rabbit warren of coffee-fuelled loveliness under Howe Street in the New Town.

Named after Joe's grandfather, the cafe is full of nods to the family's history, from the black and white photos on the menus to the retro touches – spot the vintage Singer sewing machine and bookcase of board games.

Once you've scuttled your way below pavement level, make yourself at home with a steaming bowl of soup or vibrant chunk of frittata from the daily specials board.

## INSIDER'S TIP PICK UP A BAG (OR TWO) OF ROUNTON BEANS AT THE COUNTER

With yoga bods getting bendy in the space upstairs, the Leo's lot continue to expand their clean eating options, from gluten free to green goodies. Don't sweat if you're after a not-so-wholesome wedge of gooey brownie though – the gang still churn out classic hearty dishes and homemade bakes to satiate the rumbliest of tums.

The ever-popular food offering isn't complete without a coffee, of course, and you won't be disappointed by the house blend from Rounton, fashioned into silky espresso on the handsome La Marzocco.

**ESTABLISHED**
2010

**KEY ROASTER**
Rounton
Coffee Roasters

**BREWING METHOD**
Espresso

**MACHINE**
La Marzocco

**GRINDER**
Mazzer Super Jolly

**OPENING HOURS**
**Mon-Fri**
8am-5pm
**Sat** 9am-5pm
**Sun** 9.30am-5pm

 Gluten FREE

 BEANS AVAILABLE INSTORE

 ALTERNATIVE MILK

 WIFI

 CYCLE FRIENDLY

 OUTDOOR seating

 FAMILY FRIENDLY

BRING YOUR OWN Cup

---

**www.leosbeanery.co.uk**   T: 01315 568403

f Leo's Beanery   🐦 @leosbeanery   📷 @leosbeanery

# MAP ⅔ 53. URBAN ANGEL

121 Hanover Street, Edinburgh, EH2 1DJ

You don't always find speciality spots serving food that's as delish as the coffee, but the gang at Urban Angel have cracked it. Well, they have been in the game for 14 years after all.

The baristas' handiwork is taken as seriously as the chefs' at this self-professed 'restaurant serving great coffee'. Sit down with head espresso slinger Matt and you'll soon be immersed in a world of impassioned bean-based banter while chomping on a drool-worthy dish from the all-day breakfast menu.

Development has been key to the success of this down-to-earth spot. Manager Andrea wants more than just brilliant beans; she wants passionate baristas who are keen to craft beautiful brews.

### INSIDER'S TIP
SPOT THE ORIGINAL BREAD OVEN AND RANGE FROM THE BUILDING'S FORMER GUISE AS A BAKERY

The crew work closely with North Star, recently collaborating to create an exclusive house blend and to train up the team. There's also a rotating filter offering for those looking to try something new, such as an eye-poppingly fruity Kenyan from Glen Lyon.

**ESTABLISHED**
2004

**KEY ROASTER**
North Star
Coffee Roasters

**BREWING METHOD**
Espresso,
batch brew,
cold brew

**MACHINE**
La Marzocco
Linea, Bunn
batch brewer

**GRINDER**
Ceado E37J,
Ceado E37T

**OPENING HOURS**
**Mon-Fri**
8am-5pm
**Sat-Sun**
9am-5pm

 Gluten FREE

 BEANS AVAILABLE INSTORE

 ALTERNATIVE MILK

 WIFI

 OUTDOOR seating

 FAMILY friendly

 BRING YOUR OWN Cup

---

**www.urban-angel.co.uk**   T: 01312 256215

f Urban Angel   🐦 @urbanangelcafe   📷 @urbanangel_cafe

# №54. LOWDOWN COFFEE

40 George Street, Edinburgh, EH2 2LE

**D**esign-led Lowdown is a veritable haven of visual delights. Head down the steps from bustling George Street and into a sleek, bright interior.

In the midst of this small space, an open layout encourages social interaction between sips. And there's a plethora of sippables to be explored.

The smart coffee menu showcases European greats, with Sweden's Koppi and Italy's Gardelli currently filling the double hopper of the EKK 43 to produce espresso drinks and Kalita filters.

### INSIDER'S TIP CHECK OUT THE WELL-STOCKED RETAIL SELECTION OF COFFEE, TEA AND CHOCOLATE

The choice at this multi-roaster bar is dictated by the season, and you'll find the likes of Colonna, Nømad, Per Nordby, Coffee Collective and April among the evolving guest line-up.

Good coffee and conversation is accompanied by an unfolding foodie offering. The striking cakes are still on point (rhubarb and sour cream loaf with raspberry and rose drizzle – drool) but you'll also find burgeoning savoury options on the small but perfectly formed menu that matches this lovely spot.

**ESTABLISHED**
2016

**KEY ROASTER**
Koppi, Gardelli Specialty Coffees

**BREWING METHOD**
Espresso, Kalita Wave

**MACHINE**
Slayer V3

**GRINDER**
Mahlkonig EKK 43

**OPENING HOURS**
**Mon-Fri**
8am-6pm
**Sat** 9am-6pm
**Sun** 10am-6pm

Gluten FREE

BEANS AVAILABLE INSTORE

ALTERNATIVE MILK

WIFI

CYCLE FRIENDLY

OUTDOOR SEATING

T: 01312 262132
🐦 @coffeelowdown   📷 @lowdown_coffee

# MAP№ 55. CAIRNGORM COFFEE – FREDERICK STREET

41a Frederick Street, Edinburgh, EH2 1EP

The original Cairngorm Coffee has had a bit of work done since last year's guide, with a new wood-clad counter at the heart of the snug basement just off George Street.

The refurb has allowed owner Robi Lambie and the small gang of enthusiastic baristas to push their celebration of speciality further. *'We've started pre-dosing and freezing our beans for every espresso shot before grinding,'* explains Robi. *'We decided to sink a freezer into the countertop to maximise our workflow. It's a pretty bold move but we believe the results speak for themselves.'*

### INSIDER'S TIP
**THIS IS A PERFECT PLACE TO HUNKER DOWN WITH A LAPTOP AND CATCH UP ON MAIL**

Beans from The Barn and La Cabra are among other European coffees which are now ground-to-order from frozen for the EK shot espresso bill, while notable guests on batch brew include Edinburgh roaster Obadiah.

Cairngorm's signature grilled cheese stacks still fuel busy shoppers and flagging caffeine tourists from the city centre hangout. Mobile brews are also popular – don't forget to pack your re-usable cup.

**ESTABLISHED**
2014

**KEY ROASTER**
The Barn,
La Cabra

**BREWING METHOD**
EKspresso,
batch brew

**MACHINE**
La Marzocco
Linea Classic

**GRINDER**
Mahlkonig EK 43

**OPENING HOURS**
**Mon-Fri**
8am-5pm
**Sat-Sun**
9am-5pm

---

**www.cairngormcoffee.com**  T: 01316 291420

f Cairngorm Coffee Co.  🐦 @cairngormcoffee  📷 @cairngormcoffeeco

# MAP № 56. HYDE & SON

127 George Street, Edinburgh, EH2 4JN

We'd recommend scheduling this newbie as your final stop on any coffee tour of Edinburgh, as after sampling the signature low pressure espresso you'll want to stay on for its caffeine-laced cocktails.

Pushing coffee's place on the drinks list past the conventional espresso martini, Hyde & Son's bartenders combine speciality beans with craft spirits to produce concoctions such as the Netflix and Chill: a moreish compilation of espresso, coconut syrup, coffee liqueur and ice cold milk.

### INSIDER'S TIP
**CHECK OUT THE WEEKEND EVENTS INCLUDING DJ NIGHTS AND YOGA CLASSES**

Espresso and filter (sans booze) are crafted with just as much care, overseen by head of coffee – and Coffee Masters UK champ – James Wise. London's Volcano Coffee Works is the roastery of choice, though guests such as Fortitude and Assembly are often available to sample on V60, Chemex and AeroPress.

A swift stroll from the castle, this is a stylish spot from which to refuel and plan the rest of your trip. Designers Grzywinski+Pons have done a fabulous job with the interior: check out the marble-topped, grey-tiled bar for a guaranteed Instagram hit.

ESTABLISHED
2017

KEY ROASTER
Volcano Coffee Works

BREWING METHOD
Espresso, V60, AeroPress, filter, Chemex

MACHINE
Sanremo Opera

GRINDER
Mahlkonig Peak, Mahlkonig EK 43

OPENING HOURS
**Mon-Sat**
7am-11pm
**Sun** 8am-10pm

Gluten FREE

BEANS AVAILABLE
INSTORE

ALTERNATIVE MILK

WIFI

CYCLE FRIENDLY

OUTDOOR seating

FAMILY FRIENDLY

COFFEE COURSES

---

**www.hydeandson.com** T: 01312 852050

f Hyde & Son 🐦 @hydeandson 📷 @hydeandson

# ᴹᴬᴾ**57.** CASTELLO COFFEE CO. – CASTLE STREET

7a Castle Street, Edinburgh, EH2 3AH

**S**mall but perfectly formed, the original Castello Coffee flies the flag for Edinburgh's indies at its city centre location.

From the 'independent speciality coffee house' sign on the door to the faithful locals lining up for their speciality hit, it's become a popular spot as an artisan alternative to Castle Street's corporate chains.

Inside the shoebox-sized shop there's space for a cluster of coffee fans to cosy down with a silky AllPress espresso, while outside there are a handful of seats from which to imbibe a brew with knockout castle views.

### INSIDER'S TIP CHECK OUT CASTELLO'S NEW (BIGGER) SPECIALITY SPOT 15 MINUTES AWAY IN BRUNTSFIELD

You wouldn't believe what the Castello crew manage to squeeze into this TARDIS of coffee houses though. Iced speciality drinks? Check. An array of fruit-packed smoothies? Check. Basket of baked goods on the counter? Check. Not to mention the homemade soup bubbling away in the corner, tempting lunchers in from the cold with fragrant wafts of coriander.

ESTABLISHED
2012

KEY ROASTER
AllPress
Espresso

BREWING METHOD
Espresso

MACHINE
La Marzocco
GB5

GRINDER
Nuova Simonelli
Mythos One

OPENING HOURS
**Mon-Fri**
7.30am-6pm
**Sat** 8.30am-6pm
**Sun** 10am-6pm

T: 01312 259780
f Castello Coffee Co. 🐦 @castellocoffee 📷 @castellocoffee

# 58. CAIRNGORM COFFEE – MELVILLE PLACE

1 Melville Place, Edinburgh, EH3 7PR

With a monthly changing espresso and weekly single origin on batch brew, every trip to Cairngorm's second outpost offers something novel.

The continual switch between speciality roasters – faves include The Barn, La Cabra and Obadiah – and focus on batch brew are just a couple of the small tweaks owner Robi Lambie has been making this year to keep his speciality offering at the top of its game.

**INSIDER'S TIP** REP YOUR FAVOURITE COFFEE SHOP WITH A SWEATSHIRT FROM THE MERCH COLLECTION

Another is his first foray into roasting, with his dad – and fellow coffee shop owner – Robin. The collaborative project has been brewing for a while and beans roasted in the Cairngorm hills are set to hit both of the Edinburgh cafes later this year.

While the coffee may be in constant development, the chunky grilled cheese sandwiches (phwoar), slick decor and sociable vibe that the Melville venue is loved for aren't going anywhere. Grab a stool at the panoramic windows and watch New Town's busy hubbub over a damn good brew.

**ESTABLISHED**
2016

**KEY ROASTER**
The Barn,
La Cabra

**BREWING METHOD**
Espresso,
batch brew

**MACHINE**
Sanremo Opera

**GRINDER**
Nuova Simonelli
Mythos,
Mahlkonig EK 43

**OPENING HOURS**
**Mon-Fri**
8am-6pm
**Sat-Sun**
9am-6pm

www.cairngormcoffee.com

f Cairngorm Coffee Co.   @cairngormcoffee   @cairngormcoffeeco

# №59. THE COUNTER – USHER HALL

The Police Box, McCrae's Place, Edinburgh, EH1 2DJ

A few years ago, Sally and Ali McFarlane decided to give a little love and attention to a derelict police box in Morningside. Seeing its potential, and with the ability to 'think small', they converted it into a takeaway coffee shop.

It was a hit and they went on to bag more police boxes across the city, including this one in McCrae's Place just outside the magnificent Usher Hall arts venue.

### INSIDER'S TIP PICK UP AT LEAST TWO SALTED CARAMEL COOKIES – THEY'RE ADDICTIVE

You can't sit inside (Dr Who fans take note – this is not a TARDIS) but no matter, as you can find a perch outside or simply wander off to do some exploring, eco coffee cup in hand.

Do take a peek inside while your drink's being made though, because The Counter is a work of art: with everything perfectly placed, it's simplicity itself.

Serving The Counter's own house blend from Edinburgh's Mr Eion, you'll be treated to a perfect cup that would do the most pernickety coffee geek proud.

ESTABLISHED
2015

KEY ROASTER
Mr Eion
Coffee Roaster

BREWING METHOD
Espresso

MACHINE
Zoe Compact

GRINDER
Stardust

OPENING HOURS
**Mon-Fri**
7.30am-3pm

 BEANS AVAILABLE / INSTORE

 ALTERNATIVE MILK

 CYCLE FRIENDLY

 FAMILY FRIENDLY

  DISABLED ACCESS

---

f The Counter  🐦 @thecountered  📷 @thecountered

# MAP №60. LOVECRUMBS

155 West Port, Edinburgh, EH3 9DP

Don't fool yourself that it's only going to be a quick coffee at this Edinburgh temptress: one lustful look at the contents of lovecrumbs' antique cake cabinet and you'll be putty in their flour-dusted hands.

The team of bakers and baristas have been crafting Insta-famous cakes and top-notch brews from the beautiful West Port bolthole since 2012, calling on North Berwick roaster Steampunk to keep the hopper topped up with speciality-standard beans.

Local indies such as Fortitude and Obadiah ensure that there's an alternative available on batch brew, while fellow Edinburgh baking chums from the Company Bakery collective stock the cafe with loaves for the line-up of rustic lunchtime eats.

### INSIDER'S TIP GETTING HITCHED? LET THE LOVECRUMBS GANG CREATE YOUR SWEET SHOWSTOPPER

The collaborations don't stop there; 2017 not only welcomed a brand new shop in Stockbridge but also the addition of a Century General Store concession at lovecrumbs HQ. Curating design-led homewares, magazines and stationery to browse and buy, the collection is almost as drool-worthy as the bakes.

**ESTABLISHED**
2012

**KEY ROASTER**
Steampunk Coffee

**BREWING METHOD**
Espresso, batch brew

**MACHINE**
La Marzocco Linea

**GRINDER**
Victoria Arduino Mythos One, Mahlkonig EK 43

**OPENING HOURS**
**Mon-Fri**
9am-6pm
**Sat** 9.30am-6pm
**Sun** 12pm-6pm

BEANS AVAILABLE INSTORE

ALTERNATIVE MILK

WIFI

BRING YOUR OWN Cup

---

www.lovecrumbs.co.uk   T: 01316 290626

f Lovecrumbs   🐦 @hellolovecrumbs   📷 @hellolovecrumbs

# №61. THE COUNTER ON THE CANAL

Lower Gilmore Bank, Edinburgh, EH3 9QP

The narrowboats moored up alongside Union Canal are a charming sight, but take a close look at the one with a couple of tables outside and you'll be happy to discover it's a coffee shop in disguise.

The Counter on the Canal belongs to the quirky and crowd-pleasing family of Counter coffee outposts which you'll find dotted around the city in antique police boxes.

We'd argue that taking to the water is even harder than serving drinks from a small box, but the team clearly have good sea legs as they serve a stellar espresso from their boat hatch.

### INSIDER'S TIP LINGER AWHILE AND ENJOY A COFFEE IN A DECKCHAIR, COMPLETE WITH COSY BLANKET

It's a perfect pit-stop for commuters using the towpath, or anyone seeking a peaceful waterside setting from which to enjoy a brew.

The coffee itself is the house blend created in the city by Mr Eion and is accompanied by a changing selection of homemade cakes and traybakes which are whipped up in the boat's galley kitchen.

ESTABLISHED
2016

KEY ROASTER
Mr Eion
Coffee Roaster

BREWING METHOD
Espresso

MACHINE
Zoe Compact

GRINDER
Stardust

OPENING HOURS
**Mon-Fri**
7.30am-4.30pm
**Sat-Sun**
10am-4.30pm

 f The Counter    🐦 @thecountered    📷 @thecountered

# DEVELOPED WITH BARISTAS FOR BARISTAS

- Perfect for latte art
- No added sugar
- Cholesterol free, low fat alternative to milk
- 30% less calories than skimmed & regular soy milk

Baristas know their coffee better than anyone. That's why we got baristas to help us make our new, low calorie Almond Breeze® Barista Blend. It's deliciously creamy and frothy, making it perfect for the world's finest coffee. And because it's an almond drink, it's dairy free and soya free

For more information & stockists visit **bluediamondalmonds.co.uk**

# №62. CASTELLO COFFEE CO. – BARCLAY TERRACE

7-8 Barclay Terrace, Bruntsfield, Edinburgh, EH10 4HP

Castello Coffee's second shop in Bruntsfield is like the baby brother who grew up to be 6'2".

After winning over Edinburgh locals and caffeine-seeking visitors with his little-but-lovely speciality cafe on Castle Street, Sandro del Greco decided to broaden his beanie horizons with a second spot in 2017.

The Barclay Terrace outpost fits the original Castello bill: fab food (including those irresistible homemade soups), cracking coffee and friendly faces – everything's just been scaled up.

Occupying the space of two shops, the big little brother is a labyrinth of nooks and corners in which to settle down with a coffee and a slice of cake.

## INSIDER'S TIP
**SIT BY THE WINDOWS FOR SWEET VIEWS OF MEADOWS PARK AND THE BRUNTSFIELD LINKS**

The Redchurch House blend from AllPress provides a big caramel, chocolatey hit in the line-up of espresso based drinks – an all-rounder for newbies and bean geeks alike.

And keep 'em peeled for Sandro's selection of guest roasters which are set to hit both cafes soon.

---

ESTABLISHED
2017

KEY ROASTER
AllPress
Espresso

BREWING METHOD
Espresso

MACHINE
La Marzocco
Strava AV

GRINDER
Nuova Simonelli
Mythos One

OPENING HOURS
**Mon-Fri**
7.30am-6pm
**Sat-Sun**
8.30am-6pm

 Gluten FREE

 BEANS AVAILABLE INSTORE

 ALTERNATIVE MILK

 WIFI

 CYCLE FRIENDLY

 FAMILY FRIENDLY

 DISABLED ACCESS

 BRING YOUR OWN Cup

---

T: 01312 259780

f Castello Coffee Co. 🐦 @castellocoffee 📷 @castellocoffee

# MAP № 63. ROUNDSQUARE COFFEE HOUSE

132 Morningside Road, Edinburgh, EH10 4BX

**Y**ou know you're in safe hands when the barista pulling your espresso also happens to be one of the roasters transforming the green beans into the house blend of caramely deliciousness.

At this contemporary coffee house in Morningside you'll often find Roundsquare co-founder Lucas Barraud working his magic on the snazzy Sanremo.

### INSIDER'S TIP BRUSH UP YOUR BREWING SKILLS AT ONE OF THE NEW BARISTA COURSES

Lucas and pals Heather Stevenson and Partenie McGuigan started roasting the Roundsquare blend and a rotation of single estate beans on a Probat 12 roaster, before launching their first speciality cafe in January last year. *'We pride ourselves on knowing exactly what's behind every single cup of coffee that we produce,'* says Lucas.

Join the friendly rabble of freelancers plugged in at the tall table, talk coffee with fellow caffeine fiends at the communal benches, or get a bit of me time with a lip-smackingly good pourover at the huge arch windows.

Simple brunch and lunch plates – we're all over the sourdough with cinnamon, banana and honey – keep the creative juices flowing, with sweet support in the form of countertop cakes and pastries.

**ESTABLISHED**
2017

**KEY ROASTER**
Roundsquare Roastery

**BREWING METHOD**
Espresso, pourover

**MACHINE**
Sanremo

**GRINDER**
Sanremo SR50 x 2, Mahlkonig EK 43

**OPENING HOURS**
**Mon-Fri**
8am-6pm
**Sat** 8am-7pm
**Sun** 10am-6pm

---

T: 01316 035818

f Roundsquare Coffee House  🐦 @roundsquarer  📷 @roundsquare_coffee_house

# MAP 64. THE MILKMAN

7 Cockburn Street, Edinburgh, EH1 1BP

**H**idden in plain sight, a swift walk from Waverley train station, this compact speciality cafe and espresso bar is bursting at the seams with character.

The historic – and Scottish World Heritage protected – sign above its door signals to coffee-craving commuters and locals in search of something specialist that they'll find caffeinated refuge on Cockburn Street.

The blend of original features and modern additions inside this little hub are as alluring as the slick coffee offering. Nab one of the window seats or take your coffee continental-style at a bar that's crafted from 100 year-old wood.

**INSIDER'S TIP** CHECK OUT THE RACKS OF COFFEE GEAR AND BOOKS ADORNING THE EXPOSED BRICK WALLS

Coffee charging the top-of-the-range EK 43 and Mahlkonig Peak grinders is sourced from Scottish and European roasters, and prepared with precision by the knowledgeable babble of baristas.

In summer, you'll find the crowds enjoying cold brew and diner-style milkshakes on the hill-defying alfresco seating, with plenty ditching the beach bod diet in favour of locally made gluten-free or vegan bakes.

**ESTABLISHED**
2015

**KEY ROASTER**
Five Elephant,
Dear Green
Coffee Roasters,
Obadiah

**BREWING METHOD**
Espresso,
batch brew,
AeroPress

**MACHINE**
La Marzocco
Linea Classic

**GRINDER**
Mahlkonig Peak,
Mahlkonig EK 43

**OPENING HOURS**
**Mon-Fri**
8am-6pm
**Sat-Sun**
9am-6pm

Gluten FREE

BEANS AVAILABLE
INSTORE

ALTERNATIVE MILK

WIFI

OUTDOOR seating

DISABLED ACCESS
BRING YOUR OWN cup

www.themilkman.coffee   T: 07772 077920

f The Milkman   🐦 @themilkmanedin   📷 @themilkmancoffee

# №65. HULA JUICE BAR

103-105 West Bow, Edinburgh, EH1 2JP

Photo: @wearetrouva

Imagine lying on a lounger, feeling a warm breeze steal over your body while listening to waves lapping at the shore ...

Okay, so you may not actually be in the Tropics, but you'll get transported to another place that's all relaxed, healthy holiday vibes at Hula Juice Bar.

*'We've never tried to replicate or bend to trendy coffee shop style,'* says owner and founder Susan Doherty. It's an approach that's working for the West Bow hangout, which repeatedly appears in top ten cafe lists.

### INSIDER'S TIP FOR THE FULL HAWAIIAN EXPERIENCE, TRY THE NEW LUNCHTIME POKE BOWL

In the shadow of the castle and on one of the most photographed streets in the world, Hula is bright and colourful inside; just stepping through the door brings a smile, however wet and cold it may be outside.

From breakfast onwards, you'll find hungry locals and visitors piling in for their fix of super healthy, fresh food and drink. The Hawaiian theme, with imaginative juices and beautifully presented grazing bowls, is as justifiably popular as the expertly brewed coffee and drinks list which includes an energy boosting turmeric latte.

**ESTABLISHED**
2007

**KEY ROASTER**
Artisan Roast
Coffee Roasters

**BREWING METHOD**
Espresso

**MACHINE**
La Spaziale

**GRINDER**
Mazzer Major

**OPENING HOURS**
**Mon-Sun**
8am-6pm
(extended hours
in summer)

 Gluten FREE

 BEANS AVAILABLE INSTORE

 ALTERNATIVE MILK

 WIFI

 OUTDOOR seating

 FAMILY friendly

 DISABLED ACCESS

 BRING YOUR OWN Cup

---

www.hulajuicebar.co.uk   T: 01312 201121

f Hula Juice Cafe   🐦 @hulajuicebar   📷 @hulajuicebar

# MAP № **66. BREW LAB COFFEE**

6-8 South College Street, Edinburgh, EH8 9AA

Locals love spending time in Brew Lab, so much so that co-founders Dave and Tom have extended the opening hours to create something very special.

You can now pitch up for a coffee, craft beer, glass of natural wine or cocktail (the cold brew martini is a winner) and dig into a plate of charcuterie and cheese well into the evening.

Already one of Scotland's coffee institutions – it's said to be the largest speciality coffee bar in the country – Brew Lab has morphed into a cross between a coffee shop and a bar.

### INSIDER'S TIP **GET THERE BEFORE 10AM TO ENJOY A RARE MOMENT OF QUIET WITH A POUROVER**

It works because it's been done with the same passion that first fired up Dave and Tom five years ago, when they took on an old university office on South College Street, stripped it and put in an enormous brew bar.

With weekly rotating filters, a different single origin espresso every weekend and a large range of quality guest roasters, Brew Lab is a paradise for bean geeks. It's much more than that, though, thanks to its relaxed reclaimed furniture interiors and foodie offering of artisan baguettes, soups, salads and bakery eats.

**ESTABLISHED**
2012

**KEY ROASTER**
Union Hand-Roasted Coffee

**BREWING METHOD**
Espresso, Kalita Wave, cold brew

**MACHINE**
Victoria Arduino Black Eagle gravimetric

**GRINDER**
Nuova Simonelli Mythos One

**OPENING HOURS**
**Mon-Tue**
8am-6pm
**Wed-Fri**
8am-8pm
**Sat-Sun**
9am-8pm

 *Gluten* FREE

 BEANS AVAILABLE INSTORE

 ALTERNATIVE MILK

 WIFI

 FAMILY FRIENDLY

 DISABLED ACCESS

 BRING YOUR OWN CUP

 COFFEE COURSES

---

**www.brewlabcoffee.co.uk**   T: 01316 628963

f Brew Lab Coffee   🐦 @brewlabcoffee   📷 @brewlabcoffee

# MAP №**67.** SÖDERBERG QUARTERMILE

27 Simpson Loan, Edinburgh, EH3 9GG

**B**ehind this cathedral to fika is a team of brew-crafting, baking extraordinaires, who toil from before sunrise to bring its regular crowd of lecturers, students and business folk their daily dose of authentic Swedish fare.

Söderberg's scandi roots surface in both its design and foodie offering. Nab a stool at the floor-to-ceiling windows or settle down at one of the long tables and enjoy the hygge vibe as the oven emanates toasty wafts of freshly baked, Swedish-inspired pastries.

### INSIDER'S TIP ENJOY YOUR BREW WITH A CARDAMOM BUN STRAIGHT FROM THE OVEN – SWEDEN'S FAVE FIKA

A visit wouldn't be complete without being tempted by the drool-inducing kanelbulle (cinnamon buns), palsternackskaka (parsnip cake) or rågbröd (Swedish rye). You'll need a few return trips to tick off the full smorgasbord of baked delights.

Providing an authentic coffee pairing for these baked beauties (and in keeping with the Scandi feel) is the Bella blend for espresso and Fika blend for filter from Swedish roaster, Johan & Nyström.

ESTABLISHED
2007

KEY ROASTER
Johan & Nyström

BREWING METHOD
Espresso, filter

MACHINE
La Marzocco Linea PB

GRINDER
Mahlkonig K30 Vario

OPENING HOURS
**Mon-Fri**
7.30am-6pm
**Sat-Sun**
9am-6pm

 Gluten FREE

 BEANS AVAILABLE INSTORE

 ALTE RNA TIVE MILK

 CYCLE FRIENDLY

 OUTDOOR seating

 FAMILY friendly

 DISABLED ACCESS

 BRING YOUR OWN Cup

---

**www.soderberg.uk**   T: 01312 285876

f Söderberg   ⓞ @soderbergbakery

# MAP№ 68. FILAMENT COFFEE – CLERK STREET

38 Clerk Street, Edinburgh, EH8 9HX

2017 was a big year for Filament. If launching a second shop and bringing in a new team wasn't enough of a challenge, the Edinburgh frontrunner also entered the realm of roasting.

Its new venue on East Trinity Road serves as a contemporary roastery cafe where the caffeine curious can watch the process in action, while the original coffee shop showcases Filament beans alongside some of Europe's finest roasters.

Currently, espresso and batch brew are reserved for the roastery's latest single origins while the brew bar – stocked with AeroPress and V60 – features world class roasters such as Tim Wendelboe, as well as lesser known indies including Rusty Nails.

### INSIDER'S TIP LOOK OUT FOR OSLO'S TIM WENDELBOE BEANS, AVAILABLE TO BUY IN STORE SOON

Table service is in the pipeline for later this year (*'We want people to feel they can relax while we take care of them,'* says manager Anna), though for the time being the greedy menu of filled bagels, smoothies and local bakes – check out the cinnamon buns – accompanying the coffee can be ordered at the bar.

ESTABLISHED
2013

KEY ROASTER
Filament
Coffee Roastery

BREWING METHOD
Espresso, V60,
AeroPress,
batch brew

MACHINE
Nuova Simonelli
Aurelia

GRINDER
Mythos One,
Mahlkonig EK 43

OPENING HOURS
**Mon-Fri**
7.30am-6pm
**Sat-Sun**
9am-6pm

www.filamentcoffee.com   T: 07712 218884

f Filament Coffee   @filament_roastery

# MAP №**69.** THE BEARDED BAKER

46 Rodney Street, Edinburgh, EH7 4DX

Since opening its first cafe-bakery hybrid a year ago, The Bearded Baker has continued to busily churn out the city's fave vegan cinnamon buns (and bagels, muffins, loaves and doughnuts) which charm carb-loving locals and thrill-seeking day trippers.

Peer into the teeny brightly-lit space and you won't believe the buzz of activity going on out back as bake boss Rowan creates sweet somethings for indies across the city.

### INSIDER'S TIP ARRIVE EARLY – THE CINNAMON BUNS HAVE BEEN KNOWN TO DISAPPEAR WITHIN 30 MINUTES

But it's not just Bearded Baker bagels which are satisfying the good folk of Edinburgh: the team knock up stonking drinks at their HQ too. With a mutual love of brews and bakes, the gang have collaborated on bean and doughnut swaps with local roaster Williams & Johnson.

Get in the queue (there usually is one) and choose from an espresso based or AeroPress brew to savour with your freshly-filled hot bagel or affogato doughnut.

**ESTABLISHED**
2017

**KEY ROASTER**
Williams & Johnson Coffee Co.

**BREWING METHOD**
Espresso, AeroPress

**MACHINE**
Conti X-One

**GRINDER**
Fiorenzato F83E

**OPENING HOURS**
**Mon-Fri**
7.30am-5pm
**Sat-Sun**
9am-4pm

Gluten FREE

BEANS AVAILABLE INSTORE

ALTERNATIVE MILK

WIFI

FAMILY FRIENDLY

---

**www.thebeardedbaker.co.uk**   T: 01312 819285

f The Bearded Baker   🐦 @bakerbearded   📷 @beardedbakerscot

# MAP 70. CENTURY GENERAL STORE

1-7 Montrose Terrace, Edinburgh, EH7 5DJ

Collating handsome homewares, beautiful brunch dishes and finely-crafted coffee under one turret-topped roof, this retail and cafe space on Montrose Terrace is all style – with extra substance.

Make a trip with plenty of time to browse the design-led curation of enamelware, stationery, house plants and cards, before bagging a table and sampling the equally contemporary caffeine collection.

An eclectic mix of UK roasters keeps the coffee offering fresh – look out for names such as Old Spike, Alchemy and Dark Arts stocking the guest hopper and retail shelves. *'We like to source speciality beans that you don't usually encounter in Edinburgh,'* explains co-owner and experienced barista, Niall Langlands.

### INSIDER'S TIP BRING YOUR LYCRA FOR AFTER-HOURS YOGA UPSTAIRS

Leave time to get your fill of the newly fattened brunch menu and seasonal weekend specials. Noteworthy collabs from the kitchen include picante beans and mushrooms on sourdough, along with french toast with honey-poached pears and crème fraîche – both as 'grammable as Century's open plan space.

**ESTABLISHED**
2016

**KEY ROASTER**
Assembly Coffee

**BREWING METHOD**
Espresso,
batch brew

**MACHINE**
La Marzocco
Linea Classic

**GRINDER**
Mazzer Robur E,
Anfim x 2,
Mahlkonig
Tanzania

**OPENING HOURS**
**Mon-Fri**
8am-5pm
**Sat-Sun**
9am-5pm

 Gluten FREE

 BEANS AVAILABLE INSTORE

 ALTERNATIVE MILK

 WIFI

 OUTDOOR seating

 FAMILY FRIENDLY

 DISABLED ACCESS

 BRING YOUR OWN cup

---

**www.centurygeneralstore.com**

 f Century General Store  🐦 @centurygeneral  📷 @centurygeneralstore

Working with the best food, drink, hospitality and tourism businesses.
Call us to add a pinch of salt to your
**branding, design, copywriting and magazines**

# ᴹᴬᴾ 71. THE LOFT CAFE & BAKERY

Peffer Place, Haddington, East Lothian, EH41 3DR

A light and bright top floor of an 18th century stone building is home to the appropriately named Loft Cafe.

Local provenance and seasonality are at the heart of this popular foodie destination run by Charlotte and Anita. Greedy delights are served from breakfast onwards and include classic faves and contemporary bakes, all handcrafted by Sarah and her team in the kitchen.

At lunch there's an array of house salads to choose from alongside Loft specials such as Sarah's beef stovies with oatcakes and chutney.

### INSIDER'S TIP  THERE'S A MEAN HOT CHOC MENU: TRY THE SPICE-INFUSED AZTEC

Barista Jake is responsible for the quality coffee offering which is based on Artisan Roast's Janszoon, a blend made with high altitude arabica beans from Sumatra and Brazil.

For a perfect (and slightly retro) pairing, match your brew with one of the homemade custard cream or Jammie Dodger-style biccies – best chomped outside in the sunny sheltered courtyard.

ESTABLISHED
2015

KEY ROASTER
Artisan Roast
Coffee Roasters

BREWING METHOD
Espresso,
batch brew

MACHINE
La Marzocco

GRINDER
Fiorenzato F84E,
Fiorenzato F64,
Mazzer Super
Jolly

OPENING HOURS
**Mon-Fri**
8.30am-4.30pm
**Sat** 9am-4pm

 Gluten FREE

 BEANS AVAILABLE INSTORE

 ALTERNATIVE MILK

 WIFI

 CYCLE FRIENDLY

 OUTDOOR seating

 FAMILY FRIENDLY

 DISABLED ACCESS

 BRING YOUR OWN Cup

www.loftcafebakery.co.uk   T: 01620 824456

f The Loft Café and Bakery   🐦 @loftcafebakery   📷 @loftcafebakery

# №72. STEAMPUNK COFFEE

49a Kirk Ports, North Berwick, East Lothian, EH39 4HL

**G**rab a stool at ground level and watch the roasters get to work, hunker down with a book on the mezzanine floor or secure an outdoor seat with views of the church ruins: wherever you choose to perch at this joinery-turned-roastery, there's plenty of inspiration.

Of course, it's the own-roasted coffee that really makes the experience here. Owner Catherine Franks and new head roaster Kirsty Stewart knock up an intriguing selection of single origins on the Probat roaster which the skilled baristas craft into honey-like espresso and batch brew. Beans change all the time and the two options on the La Marzocco machine often provide contrasting flavour profiles.

### INSIDER'S TIP STOCK UP ON CAFFEINE KIT, STEAMPUNK BEANS AND COFFEE MERCH FROM THE RETAIL AREA

The food is as seasonal as its coffee counterpart and a band of chefs create all the cakes, veg-laden soups and stuffed sandwiches in the glass-panelled kitchen upstairs. Swing by on a Friday evening for a late night brew and wood-fired pizza from the converted Citroën in the courtyard.

**ESTABLISHED**
2012

**KEY ROASTER**
Steampunk Coffee

**BREWING METHOD**
Espresso, Bunn batch brewer

**MACHINE**
La Marzocco Linea Classic

**GRINDER**
Mythos One

**OPENING HOURS**
**Mon-Sat**
9am-5pm
**Sun** 10am-5pm

 Gluten FREE

 BEANS AVAILABLE INSTORE

 ALTERNATIVE MILK

 WIFI

 CYCLE FRIENDLY

 OUTDOOR seating

 DISABLED ACCESS

 BRING YOUR OWN Cup

---

www.steampunkcoffee.co.uk   T: 01620 893030
**f** Steampunk Coffee   **🐦** @steampunkcoffee   **📷** @steampunkcoffee

# MAP 73. RIALTO COFFEE CO.

33 High Street, Eyemouth, Berwickshire, TD14 5EY

**W**hether you're a loyal local or just passing through on a caffeine-fuelled tour, you'll find a warm welcome at Rialto in Eyemouth.

Owners Michael and Eilyn Howes-Quintero are passionate about sharing the first-class coffee and quality food that they craft at their family cafe, ensuring every visitor leaves with a full stomach and bucket list of new beans to explore.

Bristol's Clifton Coffee provides the good stuff which Michael proudly pulls through the La Marzocco machine as silky espresso. There's usually an under-the-counter stash of guest beans too: ask nicely and he'll prepare his latest find for you in the Chemex. In summer, look out for refreshing fruity numbers available as cold brew.

**INSIDER'S TIP** SECURE A SPOT BY THE COAL FIRE AFTER A BRISK STOMP ALONG THE BERWICKSHIRE COASTAL PATH

Be sure to coincide your trip to this coastal gem with a lunchtime pit-stop as Eilyn's bowls of zesty chermoula-topped tagine, fiery empanadas and a game-changing earl grey tea loaf are worth re-routing for.

**ESTABLISHED**
2014

**KEY ROASTER**
Clifton Coffee
Roasters

**BREWING METHOD**
Espresso,
Chemex,
cold brew

**MACHINE**
La Marzocco
Linea PB

**GRINDER**
Mahlkonig
EKK 43 Twin

**OPENING HOURS**
**Tue-Sat**
9am-4pm

 Gluten FREE

 BEANS AVAILABLE INSTORE

 ALTERNATIVE MILK

 WIFI

 CYCLE FRIENDLY

 FAMILY FRIENDLY

 DISABLED ACCESS

# MAP № 74. NO 1 PEEBLES ROAD

1 Peebles Road, Innerleithen, Scottish Borders, EH44 6QX

Don't sweat about swinging by this cheerful coffee shop in muddy boots and messy scruffs, as there's a good chance you'll be cosying up at one of the communal tables with an even muddier crew of mountain bikers.

Surrounded by wooded valley walks and some of Scotland's best bike trails, Craig and Emma Anderson's bustling cafe is a hive of caffeinated activity in the sleepy town of Innerleithen.

### INSIDER'S TIP THE CHILLI HOT CHOCOLATE CARRIES A REAL KICK – IT'S NOT FOR THE FAINTHEARTED

On crisp mornings, No 1's windows mist up as early risers spill out onto alfresco seating for their pre-trail espresso fix. On return, Craig refuels lethargic limbs with velvety flat whites made from Steampunk beans, while Emma knocks up hearty toasties and breakfast stacks in the open plan kitchen.

Everyone's after the sweet spot next to the log burner, but if you can't take pole position with a blanket and wedge of something naughty from the cake cabinet, the locals swapping stories at the roomy benches are always happy to shuffle up.

**ESTABLISHED**
2014

**KEY ROASTER**
Steampunk Coffee

**BREWING METHOD**
Espresso, french press, pourover, cold brew

**MACHINE**
La Marzocco

**GRINDER**
SAB

**OPENING HOURS**
**Wed-Mon**
8am-5pm

 Gluten FREE
 BEANS AVAILABLE INSTORE
 ALTERNATIVE MILK
 WIFI
 CYCLE FRIENDLY
 OUTDOOR SEATING
 DISABLED ACCESS

**www.no1peeblesroad.coffee** T: 01896 830873
f No1 Peebles Road 🐦 @no1peeblesroad 📷 @no1_peebles_road

**49 ARTISAN ROAST COFFEE ROASTERS**

Arrow
ROASTERS & TRAINING
4

# 75. WILLIAMS & JOHNSON COFFEE CO.

MAP:

Customs Wharf, 67 Commercial Street, Edinburgh, EH6 6LH

'**W**e're a couple of geeks who know coffee,' say Zachary Williams and Todd Johnson, the brains behind the beans at the Custom Lane roastery.

The duo are being a little modest to say the least: since launching in 2016, the beans and brews have gone from strength to strength. Following meticulous sourcing and sampling, the guys have garnered a firm fanbase in the form of speciality-seeking cafes and local filter fans.

As of October 2017, the lads upped sticks and moved the roasting gear to their slick cafe: a brightly-lit beacon of caffeinated thrills inside one of the imposing stone buildings on Customs Wharf. This means all the coffee action now happens under one roof in the artsy hub by the water.

## 'WE'RE A COUPLE OF GEEKS WHO KNOW COFFEE'

A particular fave among W&J's wholesale customers is the single origin Seasonal Espresso, designed to produce a sweet, balanced and vibrant cup. And a win-win collab with The Bearded Baker means you can pick up the tastiest bagel in the city to munch on after your pourover.

**ESTABLISHED**
2016

**ROASTER**
MAKE & SIZE
Probatone
12kg

CAFE ONSITE

OPEN TO THE PUBLIC

BEANS AVAILABLE
ONLINE ONSITE

**www.williamsandjohnson.com**    T: 07932 581904

f Williams and Johnson Coffee Co.    🐦 @wjcoffee    📷 @williamsandjohnson

# MAP 76. MR EION COFFEE ROASTER

9 Dean Park Street, Edinburgh, EH4 1JN

**N**ot every neighbourhood has its own friendly bean maestro but coffee lovers in Stockbridge are spoilt to have Mr Eion (aka Eion Henderson) on hand for advice, inspiration and brewing equipment.

At this charming bean emporium you can pick up high-end seasonal blends, single origins and intriguing in-store exclusives.

Peer through the roastery window and you'll usually see Eion roasting on the bright blue Diedrich, surrounded by an array of hessian sacks brimful with greens.

Inside, you'll discover unique beans such as a distinctive tropical-fruity coffee from Myanmar. In backing a Kickstarter project with the Chin Litai farmer group, Mr Eion received one of only two bags produced for export this year.

**ESTABLISHED**
2013

**ROASTER**
MAKE & SIZE
Diedrich IR 5kg
Diedrich IR 2.5kg

**BEANS**
AVAILABLE

**OPEN**
TO THE PUBLIC

## PICK UP EVERYTHING FROM AN AEROPRESS TO A KINTO COLD BREW CARAFE

Don't fret if you can't visit in person. Eion and the friendly team (Martin, Jamie, Kelly and shop dog Mia) have launched their website from which blends such as Moustache Twirler can be ordered, so you can brew at home while tweaking your 'tache and contemplating notes of spice and dark chocolate.

**www.mreion.com**  T: 01313 431354
f Mr. Eion: Coffee Roaster  🐦 @mr_eion  @mr_eion

# MAP 77. ARTISAN ROAST COFFEE ROASTERS

Unit 4, Peffermill Business Parc, 25 King's Haugh Road, Edinburgh, EH16 5UY

**G**ustavo Pardo takes coffee seriously. And rightly so: as the first speciality coffee roaster in Scotland, Artisan Roast has ten years under its belt and is still going strong.

In fact, things only seem to get better at Artisan HQ as the clan strive to cultivate the perfect roast every time through constant development and exploration.

It all starts with meticulous sourcing by Artisan's jet-setting buyer, John Thompson, who meets quality growers around the world in search of the best beans.

Then there's the profiling, fine-tuned in the state-of-the-art lab on a two barrel Probat and 1kg Probatino; this bunch rely on nobody's cupping notes but their own.

In addition, there's a team of creative bods working hard to evolve the labels and packaging on a regular basis: *'We take the look of our packaging as seriously as the coffee,'* says Gustavo.

## ARTISAN'S CREW HAVE BEEN NAMED BEST BARISTAS IN SCOTLAND FOUR TIMES IN THE LAST SIX YEARS

This quest for perfection is benefitting others too: Artisan has collaborated with the Scottish Malawi Partnership, helping farmers increase the quality of their crop and reduce consumption of water in the growing process.

ESTABLISHED
2007

ROASTER
MAKE & SIZE
Toper 30kg
Diedrich 12kg
Probat two
barrel
Probatino 1kg

OPEN
BY APPOINTMENT

COFFEE
COURSES

COURSES

BEANS
AVAILABLE
ONLINE ONSITE

www.artisanroast.co.uk    T: 07590 590667

f Artisan Roast Coffee Roasters   🐦 @artisanroast   📷 @artisanroastcoffeeroasters

# MAP 78. COFFEE NEXUS

8 Howard Street, Edinburgh, EH3 5JP

Photo: Dori Czegledi

Master of coffee, John Thompson, has had another trailblazing year. The founder of Coffee Nexus – Scotland's only Q robusta grader and a Cup of Excellence head judge – not only spoke at the Roaster Guild of Europe camp but also co-hosted the UK Roasting Championship with Dear Green in Glasgow.

**ESTABLISHED**
2009

COFFEE COURSES

COURSES

## 'THIS YEAR WE MADE OUR FIRST TRIP TO BURUNDI AND WORKED WITH SOME STELLAR COFFEES FROM COLOMBIA'

His training and consultancy lab in the heart of Edinburgh continues to spearhead the quest for exceptional coffee, delivering ongoing support to a string of businesses.

*'This year we've bought some super tasty coffee for Artisan Roast, made our first trip to Burundi and worked with stellar coffees from Colombia in the Cup of Excellence,'* says John.

Roasteries and coffee businesses of all sizes seek out his expertise: as an SCA Education and Advisory Council member he certifies hundreds of people each year in cupping, roasting and green coffee.

---

www.coffeenexus.co.uk   T: 01315 561430

f Coffee Nexus Ltd   🐦 @coffeenexus   📷 @coffeenexus

# MAP:79. BREW LAB TRAINING LAB

6-8 South College Street, Edinburgh, EH8 9AA

t's fitting to find a barista school in the basement of Edinburgh's coffee mecca, Brew Lab.
Don't worry that it'll all be too cool for school though, as courses are designed for all levels and abilities. Hone your cupping skills and swot up on the science behind speciality at a sensory class, get hands on with V60, AeroPress and Kalita, or go the whole hog and learn the brass tacks of slinging espresso like a pro.

Kitted out with all the latest gear, the deftly-designed space includes an espresso set-up with swish VA 388 Black Eagle machine and a separate brew bar for filter frolics.

**ESTABLISHED**
2013

OPEN
BY APPOINTMENT

COFFEE
COURSES

BEANS
AVAILABLE

ONSITE

## 'SWOT UP ON THE SCIENCE BEHIND SPECIALITY AT A SENSORY CLASS'

Brew Lab has a track record of some note when it comes to coaching career baristas, and the training space is also available for pros to hire.

A gift voucher for one of these classes makes a great gift and fresh topics are always being devised (check out the new latte art class). Even better, once you've done your training you can pop upstairs to Brew Lab's new craft beer, cocktail and wine bar.

---

**www.brewlabcoffee.co.uk**   T: 01316 628963

Brew Lab Coffee   @brewlabcoffee   @brewlabcoffee

# MORE GOOD

## SO MANY EXCEPTIONAL PLACES TO DRINK COFFEE

### MAP Nº 80
## BOG MYRTLE SKYE
Bog Myrtle, Struan, Isle of Skye, IV56 8FB

**www.bogmyrtleskye.co.uk**

### MAP Nº 81
## CAFE 1925
The Old Post Office, Newton Bank,
Ardvasar, Isle of Skye, IV45 8RS

**www.cafe1925.co.uk**

### MAP Nº 82
## VELOCITY CAFE
1 Crown Avenue, Inverness, IV2 3NF

**www.velocitylove.co.uk**

### MAP Nº 83
## NETHY HOUSE CAFE & ROOMS
Nethy House, Nethy Bridge,
Inverness-shire, PH25 3EB

### MAP Nº 84
## THE CRAFTSMAN COMPANY
2 Guild Street, Aberdeen, AB11 6NE

**www.thecraftsmancompany.com**

### MAP Nº 85
## MEADOW ROAD
579 Dunbarton Road, Glasgow, G11 6HY

### MAP Nº 86
## SIEMPRE
162 Dumbarton Road, Glasgow, G11 6XE

**www.siemprebicyclecafe.com**

### MAP Nº 87
## COFFEE, CHOCOLATE AND TEA
944 Argyle Street, Glasgow, G3 8YJ

**www.maccallumsoftroon.co.uk**

## 88
### LABORATORIO ESPRESSO
93 West Nile Street, Glasgow, G1 2SH

**www.laboratorioespresso.com**

## 89
### RIVERHILL COFFEE BAR
24 Gordon Street, Glasgow, G1 3PU

**www.riverhillcafe.com**

## 90
### STAN'S STUDIO
43 Alexandra Park Street, Glasgow, G31 2UB

**www.stans-studio.com**

## 91
### BUCHTA – SPECIALITY COFFEE AND CAKES
72 Victoria Road, Glasgow, G42 7AA

**www.buchta.co.uk**

## 92
### GAMMA TRANSPORT DIVISION
6 Dean Park Street, Stockbridge, Edinburgh, EH4 1JW

**www.gammatransportdivision.com**

## 93
### SÖDERBERG STOCKBRIDGE
3 Deanhaugh Street, Edinburgh, EH4 1LU

**www.soderberg.uk**

## 94
### RONDE BICYCLE OUTFITTERS
66-68 Hamilton Place, Stockbridge, Edinburgh, EH3 5AZ

**www.rondebike.com**

## 95
### SÖDERBERG BAKERY SHOP – WEST END
31 Queensferry Street, Edinburgh, EH2 4QS

**www.soderberg.uk**

## 96
### NOIR
1 Palmerston Place, Edinburgh, EH12 5AF

**www.cafe-noir.co.uk**

## 97
### CHAPTER ONE
107/109 Dalry Road, Edinburgh, EH11 2DR

**www.chapterone.coffee**

## 98
### FIELDWORK
105 Fountainbridge, Edinburgh, EH3 9QG

**www.fieldworkcafe.co.uk**

## 99
### THE COUNTER – TOLLCROSS
Police Box, High Riggs, Tollcross, Edinburgh, EH3 9RP

## 100
### MACHINA ESPRESSO – BROUGHAM PLACE
2 Brougham Place, Tollcross, Edinburgh, EH3 9HW

**www.machina-coffee.co.uk**

## 101
### PEKOETEA
20 Leven Street, Edinburgh, EH3 9LJ

**www.pekoetea.co.uk**

## 102
### ARTISAN ROAST COFFEE ROASTERS – BRUNTSFIELD
138 Bruntsfield Place, Edinburgh, EH10 4ER

**www.artisanroast.co.uk**

## 103
### PROJECT COFFEE
192-194 Bruntsfield Place, Edinburgh, EH10 4DF

## 104
### SALT CAFE
54-56 Morningside Road, Edinburgh, EH10 4BZ

**www.salt-cafe.co.uk**

## 105
### THE COUNTER – MORNINGSIDE
Police Box, 216a Morningside Road, Edinburgh, EH10 4QQ

## 106
### BLACKWOOD COFFEE
235 Morningside Road, Edinburgh, EH10 4QT

## 107
### PAPII CAFE
101 Hanover Street, Edinburgh, EH2 1DJ

## 108
### WELLINGTON COFFEE
33a George Street, Edinburgh, EH2 2HN

## 109
### FORTITUDE COFFEE
3c York Place, Edinburgh, EH1 3EB

**www.fortitudecoffee.com**

## 110
### ARTISAN ROAST COFFEE ROASTERS – BROUGHTON STREET
57 Broughton Street, Edinburgh, EH1 3RJ

**www.artisanroast.co.uk**

## 111
### SÖDERBERG BAKERY SHOP – BROUGHTON STREET
45 Broughton Street, Edinburgh, EH1 3JU

**www.soderberg.uk**

## 112
### TWELVE TRIANGLES – BRUNSWICK STREET
90 Brunswick Street, Edinburgh, EH7 5HU

**www.twelvetriangles.com**

## 113
### PEP & FODDER
11 Waterloo Place, Edinburgh, EH1 3BG

## 114
### BABA BUDAN
Arch 12, 17 East Market Street, Edinburgh, EH8 8FS

**www.bababudan.co.uk**

## 115
### DOVECOT CAFE BY LEO'S
Dovecot Studios, 10 Infirmary Street,
Edinburgh, EH1 1LT

**www.dovecotstudios.com**

## 116
### THOMAS J WALLS
35 Forest Road, Edinburgh, EH1 2QT

## 117
### SÖDERBERG PAVILION
1 Lister Square, Edinburgh, EH3 9GL

**www.soderberg.uk**

## 118
### MACHINA ESPRESSO – NICOLSON STREET
80 Nicolson Street, Edinburgh, EH8 9EW

**www.machina-coffee.co.uk**

## 119
### KILIMANJARO COFFEE
104 Nicolson Street, Edinburgh, EH8 9EJ

## 120
### PRESS COFFEE
30 Buccleuch Street,
Edinburgh, EH8 9LP

## 121
### CULT ESPRESSO
104 Buccleuch Street, Edinburgh, EH8 9NG

**www.cult-espresso.com**

## 122
### WILLIAMS & JOHNSON COFFEE CO.
Customs Wharf, 67 Commercial Street,
Edinburgh, EH6 6LH

**www.williamsandjohnson.com**

## 123
### TWELVE TRIANGLES – PORTOBELLO HIGH STREET
300 Portobello High Street,
Edinburgh, EH15 2AS

**www.twelvetriangles.com**

## 124
### THE LITTLE GREEN VAN
North end of Bellfield Street, Portobello
Promenade, Edinburgh, EH15 2DX

# MORE GOOD Roasters

## ADDITIONAL HOT HAULS FOR YOUR HOPPER

### MAP N° 125
## SKYE ROASTERY
Cafe Sia, Broadford,
Isle of Skye, IV49 9AB

**www.cafesia.co.uk**

### MAP N° 126
## SPEYSIDE COFFEE ROASTING CO.
Garmouth Hotel, South Road, Garmouth,
Moray, IV32 7LU

**www.speysidecoffee.co.uk**

### MAP N° 127
## LOCH LOMOND COFFEE CO.
Main Street, Balmaha, Loch Lomond,
Stirling, G63 0JQ

**www.lochlomondcoffee.co.uk**

### MAP N° 128
## THE GOOD COFFEE CARTEL
12 Cornwall Street, Glasgow, G41 1AQ

**www.thegoodcoffeecartel.com**

### MAP N° 129
## CHARLIE MILLS COFFEE
Eaglesham, Glasgow, G76 0BB

**www.charliemillscoffee.com**

### MAP N° 130
## FORTITUDE COFFEE ROASTERS
Unit 6, New Broompark Business Park,
Edinburgh, EH5 1RS

**www.fortitudecoffeeroasters.com**

### MAP N° 131
## OBADIAH COLLECTIVE
Unit 6, New Broompark Business Park,
Edinburgh, EH5 1RS

**www.obadiahcollective.com**

### MAP N° 132
## FILAMENT COFFEE
44a East Trinity Road, Edinburgh, EH5 3DJ

**www.filamentcoffee.com**

### MAP N° 133
## MACHINA ESPRESSO
Unit 9, Peffermill Park, 25 Kings Haugh,
Edinburgh, EH16 5UY

**www.machina-coffee.co.uk**

### MAP N° 134
## STEAMPUNK COFFEE ROASTERS
49a Kirk Ports, North Berwick,
East Lothian, EH39 4HL

**www.steampunkcoffee.co.uk**

### MAP N° 135
## NORTHERN EDGE COFFEE
Unit 5, Meantime Workshops,
North Greenwich Road, Spittal,
Berwick-upon-Tweed, TD15 1RG

**www.northernedgecoffee.co.uk**

# MEET OUR
## committee

The *Scottish Independent Coffee Guide*'s committee is made up of a small band of leading coffee experts along with the team at Salt Media, who work with the Scottish coffee community to produce the guide

## John
### THOMPSON

John works with numerous coffee roasters, brands and farmers to improve sustainability, managing ongoing quality and adding product value. He's a head judge for the Cup of Excellence programme and strives to give producers visibility and recognition through the value chain. A regular speaker at SCA events including World of Coffee and the Roasters Guild camp, John also works within their Education Advisory Council to develop the CSP training programme.

# Lisa
## LAWSON

Lisa is a mover and shaker in the Scottish speciality coffee scene, founding Glasgow's Dear Green Coffee Roasters and kickstarting the Glasgow Coffee Festival, UK Roasting Championship and Scottish AeroPress Championship. Lisa sources beans from across the globe and turns them into beautiful coffee which she supplies to cafes and direct to home baristas. An authorised SCA trainer in sensory and barista skills, Lisa is also the chair of the membership committee of the Roaster Guild of Europe. In 2017 she was selected as one of the entrepreneurs in the Scottish Edge prize.

# Dave
## LAW

Co-owner of Brew Lab, Dave Law spent four years researching and developing the Brew Lab concept with co-founder Tom Hyde before opening the coffee bar and barista training ground in Edinburgh in 2012. He's been immersed in the industry ever since, developing Brew Lab's ready-to-drink cold brew which you'll find at stockists across the UK. When Dave's not working at the lab, you'll find him on his bike, playing music or visiting cafes around the world.

notes

Somewhere to save details of
specific brews and beans you've
enjoyed and venues visited

# Index